Songs in Waiting

Songs in Waiting

SPIRITUAL REFLECTIONS
ON CHRIST'S BIRTH

A Celebration of Middle Eastern Canticles

PAUL-GORDON CHANDLER

Unless otherwise noted, the Scripture quotations contained
herein are from the New Revised Standard Version Bible,
copyright © 1989 by the Division of Christian Education of the
National Council of Churches of Christ in the U.S.A. Used by
permission. All rights reserved.

Church Publishing
19 East 34th Street
New York, NY 10016
www.churchpublishing.org

Cover design by Corey Kent
Cover art: *The Seeing Shepherds* by Daniel Bonnell
Interior design by Vicki K. Black

Library of Congress Cataloging-in-Publication Data
Chandler, Paul-Gordon.
    Songs in waiting : spiritual reflections on Christ's birth : a
celebration of Middle Eastern canticles / Paul-Gordon Chandler.
        p.   cm.
Includes bibliographical references.
ISBN 978-0-8986-9069-9 (paperback)
1. Advent. 2. Advent music — Middle East. 3. Christmas.
4. Christmas music — Middle East. 5. Bible. N.T. Luke I-II —
Criticism, interpretation, etc. I. Title.
BV40.C455 2009
242'.332 — dc22

                                        2009008005

Printed in the United States of America

Contents

Acknowledgments

My thanks. . .

To the *congregation of the Church of St. John the Baptist/ Maadi* in Cairo, Egypt, for their constant support and listening ear to hundreds of my sermons and talks, some of which serve as the foundation for this book. I am immeasurably grateful to *Maddy Hewitt, Cabby Tennis, Barbara Jones, Maya Williamson, David Smith, Vijay Moses, Priscilla Kraut, George Tietjen,* and *Lloyd Miller* for their repeated encouragement of my preaching at St. John's.

To my many *Arab friends in the Middle East* who have helped to bring the Scriptures to life for me, as they understand their cultural context as no one else.

To the immensely gifted *Senegalese singers and musicians* whom I had the joy of listening to while growing up in West Africa, giving me a love for foreign music.

To my good friend, artist *Daniel Bonnell,* whose work always leads me to that "deeper dimension" with God, for the privilege of including four of his paintings in this book. I am honored to be a "Theo" to him.

To *Nancy Fitzgerald,* the Executive Editor of Morehouse Publishing, with whom I have been privileged to work.

And to my *family — Lynne, Britelle,* and *Treston —* for their constant and generous encouragement, assistance and support of my writing, and specifically of this book.

There are of course numerous others I could name from whose kindness and insight I have benefited, enabling me to write this short book. Suffice it to say that I am indebted to many people who have contributed to the shaping of my own spiritual journey.

The season of Advent
means there is something on the horizon
the like of which we have never seen before.
It is not possible to keep it from coming,
because it will.
That's just how Advent works.
What is possible is to not see it, to miss it,
to turn just as it brushes past you....

So stay. Sit. Linger. Tarry.
Ponder. Wait. Behold. Wonder.
There will be time enough for running.
For rushing. For worrying. For pushing.
For now, stay.
Wait.
Something is on the horizon.

—JAN L. RICHARDSON,
in *Night Visions: Searching the
Shadows of Advent and Christmas*[1]

The Surprises of God

A number of Advent seasons ago, Mustapha entered the world in the most unexpected manner. His mother was seven months pregnant, and while she had experienced a few "false" labor pains prior to her trip, she felt comfortable boarding a packed air flight from Cairo, Egypt to Addis Ababa, Ethiopia. At around twenty-five thousand feet, she started to experience severe labor pains. The flight attendants called through the loudspeaker for any doctors on the plane, and a man who had not practiced for thirteen years introduced himself with some trepidation. Upon examining her it seemed to him that she was hemorrhaging, so the pilots radioed the nearest airport, in Khartoum, Sudan, for permission to land.

1

In the meantime, the flight crew kept running warm linens between the first and economy classes, and created an airborne bed in the aisle. Soon the mother screamed loud enough for all to hear, "It's here." An eerie silence pervaded the cabin. The baby was not breathing; the umbilical cord was wrapped around his neck. Still sixty miles from Khartoum's international airport, a former paramedic on board who had some experience with infant respiratory problems came to their aid. Using a straw from a juice box, he was able to get the baby to begin breathing. The umbilical cord was then cut with shoestrings just as the plane landed. When the plane came to a stop the flight attendant announced, "It's a boy," to thunderous applause of relief and amazement. After the new mother and baby were taken off to the hospital, the plane departed on its continuing journey. All the way to Addis Ababa the flight attendants offered free drinks for all as everyone sang Arabic songs of celebration in a spirit of rejoicing.

The surprise incident on that flight to Khartoum is a vivid reminder of the dynamic of the Advent season. Advent is all about the unexpected arrival of God. Through the birth of a little boy God surprises earth with heaven.

Advent is a time when we focus on preparing for God's coming among us through the birth of the Christ Child. While Christians had begun celebrating the birth of Jesus in many places by the late second century, the tradition of setting aside the four weeks before Christmas as the season of Advent developed later, around the sixth century in the Middle East. Advent was seen as a time to look both backward and forward: backward, in celebration of the birth of Christ, and forward, with expectation of God's coming to us anew. Thus Advent is a time to celebrate the past and anticipate the future; "living in Advent" is about being in a state of readiness for the continual coming of God into our lives.

During the Advent season we are invited to prepare the way for something new in our lives, brought to us by the living God. John the Baptist, that most vocal Advent character, bursts forth out of the desert, calling us to "prepare the way for the Lord." That call actually refers to the ancient Middle Eastern custom of preparing the roads before a king traveled. When I lived in Carthage in Tunisia, North Africa, it was very clear where President Ben Ali would be traveling through the city. The police would line up along the roads hours ahead of time, positioning themselves every twenty meters or so for miles. Those roads were cleaned and new flowers were often planted. There was a sense of great anticipation; people would wait expectantly for hours for the president's imminent passing by. The way had been "prepared."

What does living in a state of "preparedness" really mean? Today we might call it being on the "lookout" for God. It's about cultivating an eternal

preoccupation with the Divine in which we find ourselves always running up the sunbeams to the Sun.
It's about cultivating a sense of wonder as we look for
God in all things. Dag Hammarskjöld, the late Sec-
retary General of the United Nations and a person of
deep faith, was instrumental in focusing on peace and
reconciliation in the Middle East. He wrote in his
diary, "We die on the day when our lives cease to be
illumined by the steady radiance, renewed daily, of a
wonder, the source of which is beyond all reason."[2]
The soul of our Christian faith is wonder. As the
renowned Christian author G. K. Chesterton wrote,
"The object of the ... spiritual life is to dig for this sun-
rise of wonder."[3]

If Advent is about training our eyes to see God's
coming, and preparing our hearts to welcome God, it
is essential that we remember that God more often
than not chooses to surprise us about the exact nature of the arrival. God is a God of the unexpected,
and being alert to the unexpected is fundamental
when we're on the lookout for God. Flannery
O'Connor, the great Catholic novelist, wrote, "From
my experience ... I have discovered that what is
needed is an action that is totally unexpected."[4] As we
prepare for the Christmas celebration during Advent,
we are reminded that there is probably no other time
of year when the theme of surprise is more evident
than the Christmas season. Everyone seems to be surprising everyone else: hence the desire to keep our

gifts to others a secret. There is something inherent in Western culture, especially in the United States, that values—and enjoys—the thrill of the surprise.

The element of surprise is also inherent in the literature of the Arab world. Consider the Arab classic *Arabian Nights Entertainments* (often referred to as "1001 Arabian Nights"), for example, which has captured the Western imagination as well. Its pages tell of the Emperor Shahriar, who is convinced that all women are treacherous, so he vows to marry a new woman every day and execute her the next morning. One day, a young Arab woman named Scheherazade is selected to marry the Emperor. To delay her inevitable execution, she tells the emperor a story of interlinking tales for 1001 nights, and his curiosity keeps Scheherazade's death at bay. (It is from these stories that we have received popular fables like *Ali Baba and the Forty Thieves, Sinbad the Sailor, King of the Black Isles*, and *Aladdin*.) Each story is filled with surprise, leaving the emperor eagerly anticipating the next day's story, until he eventually falls in love with the clever storyteller.

Life seems to go from one surprise to the next. We may find ourselves surprised about the jobs we have ended up doing, the person we married, or the place we happen to be living. A quick reading of the newspaper headlines on any given day reminds us that life is like a continuing cycle of the unexpected.

The nativity story, as presented by Matthew and Luke in their gospel accounts, sets the stage for the mood of surprise in the holiday season. While the Bible is full of examples of God surprising men and women with his faithfulness, demonstrating the very heart of God, there is perhaps no other section of the Christian Scriptures where we see God surprising so many different types of people in diverse life situations than the first two chapters of Luke's gospel. Approaching the nativity story through this lens of surprise provides freshness to this all-too-familiar story and gives new meaning to the Advent and Christmas season, opening a window for us on the mystery of God.

All through Luke's nativity narrative his characters are constantly being surprised—both by what God is doing for them and by what God has in store for their lives: Zechariah is literally struck speechless when the angel in the temple tells him he is to have a child, a son who will prepare the way for the Messiah. Mary too gets a big surprise, when she is approached one calm evening by an angel telling her she will be the mother of the Messiah. The shepherds fall to the ground in alarm at the host of angels who crowd the sky around them announcing Christ's birth. And on one seemingly normal day at the temple, Simeon sees the Christ Child for whom he has been waiting all his life. Luke's gospel is filled with other surprised characters as well: Joseph, Elizabeth, the wise men, and Anna.

Advent and Christmas are seasons of surprises. They are also seasons of singing: God's surprises are nowhere more evident than in the songs Luke shares with us that were sung surrounding the birth of the Christ Child. Perhaps Luke was a music lover, as he chooses to tell us of Christ's birth through the medium of song. His nativity narrative includes four canticles that have become some of the most important songs of the Christian faith: the *Magnificat*, or Song of Mary; the *Benedictus*, or Song of Zechariah; the *Gloria*, or Song of the Angels to the Shepherds; and the *Nunc Dimittis*, or Song of Simeon.

To understand the meaning of these canticles most fully, we need to remember that our faith is Middle Eastern in origin. The Middle East is where Christians came from, and it was only later that the center of gravity of the Christian faith moved, over the centuries, to the West. When we forget that the Christian faith was originally Middle Eastern in orientation we lose our true sense of identity: the richness of who we really are. Today most Christians in the Middle East are members of historic churches whose roots go back to Jesus' ministry, the original twelve disciples, and the first Pentecost in the church. I have friends who can trace their lineage to ancestors who heard Peter preach at Pentecost—indeed, Arab Christians are the direct descendants of these Pentecost believers, with much to teach us from their rich heritage of faith and experience over the last two thousand years. Christians in the Middle East have carried on an unbroken faithful witness to the teachings of Christ since the first century, often under the most difficult circumstances on earth.

We must also remember that the Bible, in its entirety, is an ancient Middle Eastern book — or, more accurately, a collection of ancient Middle Eastern books bound together in one volume for our benefit. Written in three Middle Eastern languages, from a diverse array of cultures and representing thousands of years of Middle Eastern history, our Bible is indeed one of the most complex volumes of Eastern literature to interpret. In order truly to understand its content, we must see it through the cultural lens of the Middle East. We are so accustomed to singing the songs of the nativity given to us by Luke as canticles and hymns in our Western liturgies, we all too easily forget that these songs are ancient Middle Eastern songs, fully embodying the region's first-century culture — as well as many elements of Middle Eastern culture today, which in many ways has remained quite unchanged.

I grew up in the Muslim country of Senegal, West Africa, and I remember with great fondness my friend Babacar Lo, a.k.a. BL. Babacar was the youngest of three brothers who lived near us, and he was the celebrated singer and chanter of our neighborhood. For

every Muslim religious festival, such as Aid al-Fitr
and Aid al-Adha, or for major celebrations, such as
the birth of a child, Babacar was selected to sing
songs of rejoicing for all in attendance. His melodi-
ous voice, whether in Wolof, the local language, or
Qur'anic Arabic, would echo throughout the neighborhood, drawing our attention to the goodness of
God.

Arabic music carries a strong dimension of surprise to the Western ear. In addition to the "foreign"
sounds of Middle Eastern musical instruments, Western listeners must adapt to the double harmonic
major scale, whose gaps evoke "exotic" music to their
ears. The main contrast between the Western chro-
matic scale and the Arabic scales is the existence of
many in-between notes, which are sometimes referred
to as quarter tones, for the sake of simplicity, using
"half-flat" or "half-sharp" as a designation for these
in-between flats and sharps.

There is very little difference between the music
of Arab Christians and Muslims. While in Cairo,
Egypt, I once received a telephone call from a friend
in the United States while watching a televised Coptic Orthodox Church's Easter Eve vigil service. My
friend, who was familiar with the Middle East, was
confused when he heard the chanting in the background coming from the television set, and asked,
"Why is the mosque call taking place in the middle of
the night?" When I informed him that it was actually

the chanting of Coptic priests, we both remarked how amazingly similar the sound was to the muezzin's call from the minaret.

Like ancient Hebrew music, much of Arabic music today is monophonic—without harmony. When Arabs play on different instruments and sing at the same time, almost the same melody is heard from each musician. Similarly, the contexts of the *Magnificat, Benedictus, Gloria,* and *Nunc Dimittis* are varied, and form quite different responses to the birth of the Christ Child. However, the songs are essentially alike in that they originate out of the surprises of God in their author's lives, with the common thread of Mary, Zechariah, the angels, and Simeon singing about the overwhelmingly beautiful nature of God.

Each of the four canticles reminds us that God surprises us when we least expect it, usually when we are in the midst of a difficult time. These songs teach us that it is in the midst of the most trying of situations that, more often than not, God surprises us with his overwhelming faithfulness. The entire nativity narrative is a compilation of stories of individuals in immensely discouraging circumstances who were surprised by God and by God's actions toward them. It is in the greatest hardships of their lives—genuine "wilderness experiences"—that God comes to surprise them. There is a wonderful Arab proverb that perhaps best captures this thought: "The further you go into the desert, the closer you come to God." The beauty of wilderness experiences is that they can represent the place where God brings deliverance. That is why the Sinai desert of Egypt had such spiritual significance for the children of Israel throughout the Scriptures: it was where God came repeatedly to their rescue. These ancient Middle Eastern Advent songs remind us that regardless of our life situations, regardless of what we are experiencing now or what we will face in the future, God always desires to overwhelm us with divine faithfulness, surprising us when we expect it least and yet need God most.

The historic church in Egypt is the Coptic Orthodox Church, believed to have been founded in the first century by the gospel writer Saint Mark. Since then, Coptic Christians have undergone tremendous challenges, from intense persecution during the pre-Islamic period to the difficulties of being the minority faith in their country, as they are today. At the heart of Coptic spirituality is the story of the Holy Family's flight to Egypt to take refuge from King Herod's order to murder all the young children in and around Bethlehem. Throughout Egypt one can visit sites where it is believed that Mary, Joseph, and the Christ Child stopped, rested, and stayed during their exile. Very near our church in Cairo is a Coptic monastery built on the site where the Copts believe the Holy Family crossed the Nile to safety as they headed to Upper Egypt. For centuries, the Holy Family's journey throughout their country has brought profound

encouragement to Copts during times of great hardship, for it lays the foundation for the way they understand God. This is illustrated in all the Coptic
icons of the Holy Family's flight to Egypt. In each
there is always an angel or dove portrayed hovering
above them as they journey through the desert, representing the saving and protecting presence of God.

In many ways these four songs given to us in
Luke's gospel all speak to the irony of God's surprises, because they really shouldn't be surprises at
all. God's surprises fill the Scriptures, and they are
simply the fulfillment of divine, beautiful promises —
the acting out of that which God has already assured
us he will do, revealing God's nature and character.
God is in the business of renewing, healing, restoring, saving, liberating, and giving us new beginnings.
And just as the angel or dove hovers above the Holy
Family in the Coptic icons throughout their journey,
so too God's protecting presence goes with us
throughout our lives.

My first visit to Saint Anthony's monastery in
Egypt, located near the Red Sea and the oldest
monastery in the world, was a powerful experience.
At that time the many ancient frescoes in the church
were being restored. For centuries, millennia of ac-
cumulated dirt, graffiti, and other markings had ren-
dered these remarkable paintings all but invisible. But
the work of restoration was revealing frescoes of
breathtaking color and beauty. In much the same

way, our careful look at the four songs in Luke's gospel will show us that God's surprises are always much more perfect and wonderful than we could ever have imagined.

Artists throughout the centuries have portrayed these songs in a multitude of mediums and genres, attempting to express their depth and power. The respected British author and theologian Alister McGrath draws in his book *The Christian Vision of God* on the works of seven renowned artists — six historical and one contemporary — to help us experience the presence and power of our loving and living God. McGrath incorporates the works of Klimt, Rembrandt, Morazzone, William Blake, Botticelli, and Rublev in his portrayal of the Christian vision of God. The contemporary artist is the well-known painter Daniel Bonnell, whose work I am honored to include in this book. Daniel is a close friend, and I have been an active and eager collector of his work from the beginning. His paintings are profoundly spiritual, and his use of color, light, and feeling is not only beautiful and emotive, but also inspired, taking the viewer to a deeper dimension. When meditating on Daniel's four paintings of these songs, I resonate with what the Russian novelist Alexander Solzhenitsyn wrote in his Nobel Prize acceptance speech, "Through art we...glimpse the Inaccessible.... And [our] soul cries out for it."

Each of these canticles is for all intents and purposes a song of adoration. Each reminds us that the natural response to God's wonderful surprises is adoration. Mary's *Magnificat* proclaims, "My soul glorifies the Lord and my spirit rejoices in God my Savior"; Zechariah's *Benedictus* begins, "Praise be to the Lord"; the angels sing the *Gloria* to the shepherds in praise to God for Christ's birth, and those shepherds, we are told, returned to their fields "glorifying and praising God"; and Simeon, upon finally seeing the Christ Child, takes him in his arms and praises God by singing what became our *Nunc Dimittis*.

The English writer C. S. Lewis put it this way: "I have tried, since that moment, to make every pleasure into a channel of adoration.... One obstacle is inattention. Another is the wrong kind of attention.... — ignor[ing] the smell of Deity that hangs about it."[5] Certainly, God comes to us in every way imaginable. When visiting Damascus, Syria during the Christmas season, I was reminded of that Eastern Advent hymn of adoration from the historic Syrian Orthodox Church titled "Praise to the Eternal Light of Love."

> Praise to the divine Light
> Praise to the Light of Light
> Praise to the Light of Life
> Praise to the Light of the world
> Praise to our Light
> Eternal Light, shining beyond the heavens,
>   radiant Son, even into our very hearts.

You illumine our lives, allowing us to see You
You enlighten us allowing us to know You
You came to dispel the darkness of our lives
Thank you for coming to enlighten us
  to the splendor of Your Love.

The seasons of Advent and Christmas remind us to learn to look for God, and give us an opportunity to fully welcome his coming anew in our lives. We are able to venture into these seasons with great confidence, for as Blaise Pascal once wrote, "Whoever looks for God has found him." As we look at these four ancient Middle Eastern Advent songs, we are reminded that God loves to surprise us when we are most in need of divine help, and that in so doing, provides surprises that are so much more wonderful than we could ever have imagined. In fact, God often chooses to bring hope and healing through the last imaginable channel. And like Mary, Zechariah, the angels, and Simeon, we cannot help but stand amazed, adoring God all the more. May God surprise each of us anew this Advent and Christmas season, as perhaps never before.

The Annunciation by Daniel Bonnell

The Annunciation

by Daniel Bonnell

In this painting we see Mary in humility wearing a rag-type gown. Her posture is also one of humility, with her hands by her side, completely defenseless before this heavenly creature. Gabriel is filled with awe at the story that he must deliver. There are two large hands that symbolize God the Father; they cradle Mary the servant.

A word on my art:

> The written word is inexpressible.
> In silence we worship the unutterable.
> In seeing the eternal, I attempt to paint
> what cannot be seen.

Chapter One

A Call to Childlikeness

THE *MAGNIFICAT, or*
SONG OF MARY

At that time Mary got ready and hurried to a town in the hill country of Judea, where she entered Zechariah's home and greeted Elizabeth. When Elizabeth heard Mary's greeting, the baby leaped in her womb, and Elizabeth was filled with the Holy Spirit. In a loud voice she exclaimed: "Blessed are you among women, and blessed is the child you will bear! But why am I so favored, that the mother of my Lord should come to me? As soon as the sound of your greeting reached my ears, the baby in my womb leaped for joy. Blessed is she

who has believed that what the Lord has said to
her will be accomplished!" And Mary said:
    "My soul glorifies the Lord
      and my spirit rejoices in God my Savior,
    for he has been mindful
      of the humble state of his servant.
    From now on all generations
      will call me blessed,
    for the Mighty One has done great things
      for me — holy is his name.
    His mercy extends to those who fear him,
      from generation to generation.
    He has performed mighty deeds
      with his arm;
    he has scattered those who are proud in
      their inmost thoughts.
    He has brought down rulers from
        their thrones
      but has lifted up the humble.
    He has filled the hungry with good things
      but has sent the rich away empty.
    He has helped his servant Israel,
      remembering to be merciful
    to Abraham and his descendants forever,
      even as he said to our fathers."
Mary stayed with Elizabeth for about three
months and then returned home.
                           (Luke 1:39–56)

When we stop to think about it, the Christmas season, especially our Western holiday celebrations of it, is essentially about and for children: Santa Claus and elves, sleighs and reindeer, Frosty the Snowman, children's Christmas pageants, gifts, stockings, tree decorating, and so on. And for the adults, what often makes our own Christmas magical is reliving our own childhood Christmas memories.

Christmas is even about being childlike, with adults putting on long white beards and dressing up like Santa Claus, or at least wearing those ridiculous Santa hats, pretending to believe in a world where elves make toys for children and a kind grandfatherly figure flies through the sky in a sleigh to deliver them, living in our imaginations for a season, and witlessly singing those joyful Christmas carols. In fact, Christmas without children around, in one way or another, would not fully seem like Christmas.

In the nativity story as told by Luke we are given the beautiful and poetic song voiced by Mary, the mother-to-be of the Christ Child, that over the centuries has been called in the liturgical church tradition the *Magnificat*. It is a song that speaks profoundly about being "childlike." Luke focuses his entire Christmas narrative around the person of Mary, who was probably just a child, a young girl who was perhaps twelve to fourteen years old, as it was customary for Jewish girls to marry just after puberty. In his book *Wishful Thinking* the novelist Frederick Buech-

ner writes from the angel Gabriel's point of view, with
the angel musing that Mary was "hardly old enough
to have a child at all, let alone this child."

In this light, the Christmas story is of a child having The Child. And when this baby named Jesus
grows up, he turns out to love children himself, giving them his utmost attention. He sits with children,
enjoys their play, and expends tremendous love, concern, and time on them. When people begin to bring
their children to Jesus for his blessing, the disciples
send them away, seeing the children as a waste of his
precious time. But Jesus rebukes them, saying, "Let
the little children come to me, and do not hinder
them, for the kingdom of heaven belongs to such as
these" (Matthew 19:14). He is saying that the deepest spiritual knowledge, while hidden from the wise
and learned, is revealed to children. He even goes so
far as to say that in order to enter the kingdom of
heaven, we must become like children: "Unless you
change and become like little children, you will never
enter the kingdom of heaven" (Matthew 18:3). Jesus
often refers to us all as "children of God"—and so we
are.

Throughout the centuries, history, tradition, and
the arts have attempted through various mediums to
portray the importance of "childlikeness." One of the
most well-known artistic renderings of the angel
Gabriel's announcement to Mary that she will be the
mother of the Christ Child was painted by Leonardo

Da Vinci while in his youth, and today is found in the Louvre in Paris. It was a child's voice that Saint Augustine heard in the year 386 in his Milan garden say of the nearby copy of the Scriptures, *Tolle lege,* "Take it up and read," which resulted in his coming to faith in Christ. We find Shakespeare frequently presenting children or youth as truly being the wisest of all, such as the characters of Macduff in *Macbeth* and the Young Prince of York in *Richard III.* Victorian literature is commonly known for its sentimental view of the significance of children. Just the name Charles Dickens summons image after image in his novels of the importance of the lives of children.

The biblical Christmas story gives much attention to Jesus' childhood. The focus of Matthew's and Luke's narratives of the nativity revolves around children: young Mary and her relative Elizabeth are both "with child"; John the Baptist and his cousin Jesus are born; the shepherds and wisemen come to see the Christ Child. We have accounts of the naming of John and Jesus, and we are told about how Simeon and Anna at the temple had waited all of their lives to see the child Messiah. However, the virtue of childlikeness in the Scriptures is nowhere more evident than in the *Magnificat,* this Song of Mary, sung by a child about a child.

The name *Magnificat* comes from the first word in the Latin Vulgate translation of this song, "magnify" or "glorify." Most probably a compilation of phrases from the Psalms, various Old Testament prophetic books, and Hannah's Song in 1 Samuel, the *Magnificat* has been part of Christian liturgy at least since the time of Saint Benedict in the fifth and sixth centuries. In the Eastern Church it is often used in the morning office, while in the West it is primarily recited during vespers or evening prayer. Within the Anglican/Episcopal Church, it is one of the canticles read or sung at Evening Prayer in the *Book of Common Prayer.*

During a recent visit with our Palestinian friend Elias Chacour, the Archbishop of Galilee and the Holy Land for the Melkite Catholic Church, which is the largest Christian body in Palestine and Israel, and the author of *Blood Brothers,* I shared with him that I was writing this chapter on the *Magnificat.* He immediately came to life and explained how expressive of Middle Eastern culture the singing of something like Mary's song still is today. While growing up in Galilee, he remembers how his mother and other women, during a celebration such as a marriage, would burst out in an extemporaneous song that no one had heard before, as an expression of rejoicing. And at the beginning of each sung verse, they would first call out in Arabic, "Pay attention."

The *Magnificat* has been recited every day for centuries by Christians, chanted by monks, and set to music by composers of every age, perhaps the most famous being Johann Sebastian Bach's composition, which he wrote for Christmas Day 1723. This famous

Song of Mary is directly occasioned by the Annunciation, the angel Gabriel's message to Mary that she
would have a son, who was to be the Messiah.

The story of how Jesus came into the world has
been communicated, mulled over, analyzed, ex-
pounded, and illustrated more than any other in
human history. This story has inspired some of the
noblest lives, and much of the greatest art, literature,
music, and architecture. It is on behalf of this baby
that majestic buildings like Notre Dame Cathedral in
Paris have been constructed and great saints like
Francis of Assisi or Mother Teresa have so whole-
heartedly dedicated their lives to the service of God
and humankind. It is to the glory of the one whose
birth we celebrate that Bach composed, El Greco
painted, Augustine of Hippo preached, and Pascal
wrote, and because Jesus the Christ was born countless individuals would receive comfort as they went
serenely to their martyrdom years after his own
death. Knowing all this, it is a deeply moving experience to stand today in Nazareth, in the Church of the
Annunciation, the site where it is believed Mary was
first confronted by the angel. The lines in the first
scene of Shakespeare's *Hamlet* seem to say it best: "So
hallowed and so gracious is the time."

At the heart of this momentous event, the child
Mary is singing a song about a child. An exceptional
young girl, chosen to be the Mother of this child Messiah, she is called in tradition *Theotokos*, the God-

bearer. The song she sings about a child has never stopped echoing down through the ages in Christendom. However, more than just being a song of a child about a child, this song is a call to each of us who desire to be followers of Christ, leading us toward becoming more childlike in our responses and relationship with our Creator. Out of the depth of her joy, Mary sings of the crucial qualities of childlikeness that the Christ Child, when he became an adult, urged his followers to embrace.

Believing

Mary begins her private and exuberant song singing, "My soul glorifies the Lord and my spirit rejoices in God my Savior." She obviously believes in this whole wild, preposterous, and seemingly crazy story that she, a virgin, is now pregnant—and not only that, but with the Messiah, the Savior for whom her people have been waiting for centuries to be revealed. Her song is actually a direct response to her relative Elizabeth's statement to her, "Blessed is she who has believed that what the Lord has said to her will be accomplished!"

Martin Luther, the fifteenth-century reformer, once said, "There are three miracles of the Nativity.

That God became man, that a virgin conceived, and that Mary believed. And the greatest of these was the last."[6] Mary is a supremely great figure, unrivaled in importance within historic Christianity. And it is proper to hold her in very high esteem, for in this young Middle Eastern girl there was great faith. At the same time, we diminish her greatness if we put her on too high a pedestal. She was just a young girl from an ordinary little town from the back of beyond; yet she believed it all.

Children have the fathomless ability to believe anything; it is one of their most beautiful traits. They haven't made up their minds yet about what is and what is not possible. Children have few fixed preconceptions about reality. If someone tells a child that under a particular bush is a magic place, they will search for it when no one is looking.

As children we lived in a summery green world where everything was possible, where in the end the villain or wicked witch was always slain and the princess rescued from her tower. Like a child, Mary quietly and simply believed. She didn't fully understand the angel's message, but she understood who God was, and she remembered the last thing the angel Gabriel said to her: "For nothing is impossible with God." Her "yes" turned the course of history.

Nevertheless, in spite of her great faith, Mary still needed reassurance. Perhaps this is why the angel told her about Elizabeth, her elderly relative who was

also inexplicably pregnant. It wasn't until she saw
Elizabeth, who astonishingly already knew about
Mary's condition, that it all came together in Mary's
young mind, and then she sings this song with all her
heart. Even for Mary, the Mother of the Christ, her
"yes" was not blind faith. Rather, like us, she had to
ponder and work through her mind all that the angel
had told her would come to pass.

Furthermore, Mary's faith as expressed in the
Magnificat did not negate the need to ask the hard
questions. Mary boldly asked the angel, "How is it all
going to happen?" She was wholly confused. And
children are fond of asking questions — outrageous
ones, sometimes. Why is the grass green? Where does
a pet go when it dies? However, the amazing thing is
that a child is open to whatever the answer is, and
often it is the adults who give answers more outrageous than the questions.

Mary was mystified, uncomprehending, and totally puzzled. While she needed divine reassurance,
with the encouragement God provided her through
Elizabeth's experience, she chooses to believe. The
Christmas story is one of impossibilities, for almost
each event goes against human logic. Yet each is
matched with ordinary individuals in the story who
choose to believe. All of them, albeit with tremendous
hesitancy at times, choose to believe the incredible.
Mary understood the greatness of God's power to
transform her ordinary human life.

It is a beautiful thing to see individuals today who, like Mary, consciously attempt not to put God into the box of their predetermined understanding of who God is and what God does or does not do, but who simply instead choose to "believe." The promise from Mary in her song is that those who do not restrict God's activity in their lives will never be the same. The ability to believe is the most striking childlike quality. In Lewis Carroll's children's classic *Through the Looking Glass,* the White Queen advises Alice to practice believing six impossible things before breakfast every day. We would all do well to take the same advice this season.

Receiving

Mary continues singing in her song:

> for he has been mindful of the humble state
>   of his servant....
> for the Mighty One has done great things
>   for me — holy is his name.

She is giving us what is called in literature a contrasted parallelism. First, Mary speaks of her "humble" state, and classifies herself a servant. Yet in the next verse she sings about the "great" things God has

done for her, that God has given *her.* These "great
things" given her by God are contrasted with her
"low or humble" status in society, making sure to emphasize her feeling of not deserving such a great gift.
The terms "humble" or "low estate" at that time had
the connotation of "poverty," both economical and so-
cietal. In other words, Mary is drawing our attention
to her state of powerlessness and maybe even cultural
oppression. She was very young, and came from
Nazareth, a town of negative reputation, considered
entirely unimportant.

Additionally, she was also a woman — a characteristic that in her day the religious leaders would view
as making an individual unlikely to be used or chosen
by God. In his morning prayers a Jewish man would
thank God he was not made "a gentile, slave, or
woman." Perhaps this is why Luke gives women a
very significant place in his gospel account: Luke sees
women as full recipients of God's love, and therefore
writes about many of them. He is the one who tells of
the sisters Mary and Martha, of Mary Magdalene,
Joanna, Susanna, the widow of Nain, the woman
who anoints Jesus' feet, the crippled woman Jesus
healed, the widow who gave all she had into the temple treasury, and the women who lamented for Jesus
as he went to the cross. It is in Luke's gospel that we
see women as subjects in some of Jesus' parables,
such as in the stories of the lost coin and the unjust
judge. Luke, a gentile (that is, a non-Jew), was pos-

sibly from Macedonia, where women held a more emancipated position, and therefore he attempts to portray God's perspective of equality in his narrative of Christ's life. However, nowhere is this more evident than in Luke's nativity narrative, where he centers the story completely around Mary, including the stories of Elizabeth her relative and Anna the prophetess in the temple. In contrast, the other primary nativity narrative, given to us by Matthew, focuses the story around Joseph.

Mary's song emphasizes God's incredible gift to her in spite of her vulnerable state and feeling of low importance. God, knowing her lowliness, bestowed on her the inestimable privilege that in her womb the Incarnation happens. In fact, she is glorying in it all; it is as if she is even boasting, saying, "He has chosen *me* for this honor, despite my poverty, obscurity, unimportance, and lowliness." Mary clearly knows how to receive from God, regardless of any feeling on her part of "undeservedness."

Certainly one characteristic of children is that they know how to accept a gift, and this is never more evident than during the Christmas season. Children don't worry about losing their dignity or becoming indebted if they accept a gift. Their conscience doesn't bother them if the gift is free; they aren't concerned about whether they deserve it or not. They just take it and receive it with joy. Most children will accept the most extravagant gifts simply because they are

given to them. More often than not, if they see something that they want very much, they will even
unashamedly ask for it. In short, children know how
to accept gifts, and fully embody the innocence and
naiveté of receiving.

Mary's song demonstrates that she also knew how
to receive, and that she didn't let all her "background"
or "baggage" get in the way of embracing the good
gifts God had for her. If you have seen Leonardo da
Vinci's beautiful painting *The Annunciation,* you may
recall how Mary is portrayed with her head lowered,
indicating her "humble state." Yet, it is while she is in
that position we see the angel Gabriel blessing her
with the sign of the cross.

The spiritual theme of the Advent and Christmas
seasons relates to the giving of ourselves anew to
God. But perhaps even more profoundly, these seasons are about receiving from God. Mary reminds us
that regardless of our abilities or inabilities, our background and past mistakes, our weaknesses, struggles,
and doubts, nothing limits or prevents God from giving to us. Mary's song infers that, paradoxically, it is
almost *because* of these things that God gives to us all
the more. Mary's childlike challenge to us in this season is to come with open hands and let God give
God's gifts to each of us anew, albeit in different
ways, with different wrappings.

When we were living in the Muslim country of
Tunisia while working with the Anglican Church, we

coordinated the first ever Tunisian "Living Christmas Pageant," complete with desert camels and their Berber guides, authentic Tunisian shepherds and their flocks of sheep, live chickens, and, of course, a newborn baby. It was seen as a raving success by Tunisian Muslims and expatriate Christians alike, and was most probably the largest Christian-sponsored public event in the country for the last seven hundred years or so.

Everyone thought the program went smoothly. However, little did they know that behind the scenes on that bitter cold December evening everything was on the verge of completely unraveling. The camels were nasty and biting the youth from the church who were riding them. Someone had unwisely tied the chickens to the rope they were perched on, and when the wind blew they were left dangling upside down by their legs. While we were singing carols, a young lamb was birthed right on stage. And to top it all off, the newborn "Christ Child" decided not to make an appearance that night, so we had to search for a substitute at the last second. And yet while from our perspective the event was just short of absolute chaos and seemed to be falling apart, to all who attended, both Christian and Muslim, it was a wonderful reminder of God's beautiful character.

Trusting and Following

Mary's song continues with her singing at the top of her voice:

> He has performed mighty deeds with his arm;
> he has scattered those who are proud in their
>   inmost thoughts.
> He has brought down rulers from their
>   thrones but has lifted up the humble.
> He has filled the hungry with good things
>   but has sent the rich away empty.

In essence, she is singing about a new way forward, or more accurately about following a new way. The words of Mary's song speak of a Messiah coming to bring about a complete reversal of human values. This Messiah, this Christ, will demonstrate that it isn't the proud or mighty or rich who have the last word. There is even a revolutionary note about filling the hungry and sending the rich away empty. During Mary's time, the religious worldview accepted that the rich would be well cared for by God, but that the poor must expect to be hungry.

She is singing of a Messiah, whom she personalizes as "her" Savior, and who turns the attitudes and orders of society upside down: morally, socially, and

economically. In this regard, the *Magnificat* challenges
the existing order; E. Stanley Jones, the famous
Methodist minister in India in the early twentieth
century and a close friend to Gandhi, once called it
"the most revolutionary of documents in the world."
The *Magnificat* was one of the foundational texts used
by those who began the liberation theology movement in Latin America, justifying revolution and the
use of military power to overthrow unjust governments and to bring justice and equality in the name of
Christ. And it is in this context that Mary refers to
God as a Savior who remembers "to be merciful."

Mary is in effect simply echoing a previous commitment she made to the angel Gabriel when she responded, "I am the Lord's servant. May it be to me as
you have said." In calling herself "the Lord's servant,"
she is meaning literally a "bonded servant" to God.
Submitting to God's way of doing things, Mary be-
comes the first disciple of the one she is carrying
within her. Luke in his gospel portrays her as the ultimate example of following God, for she expresses
her complete commitment, which at its core entails
total trust in God.

As Mary was not yet fully married, but only be-
trothed, to Joseph her husband-to-be, choosing to believe this preposterous story could easily have
resulted in great difficulty for her personally. She was
unsure of Joseph's reaction, and she probably knew
that in that time of religious legalism it was quite pos-

sible that the death penalty would be exercised against her for marital unfaithfulness. However, in spite of the potential consequences, Mary agreed to go along with the angel's proposal in simple trust, and that trust in God led her to follow a new way — God's way — of approaching life and its challenges. Children, perhaps more than anyone else, know how to trust; consequently, they are more easily able to follow completely those they trust. As a parent, you can wake your children up in the middle of night, in complete darkness, and ask them to follow you. And, in the darkness, they will let you lead them wherever you choose, so complete is their trust in you.

Mary, in singing these powerful "revolutionary" words, is saying she trusts her Savior and will follow his new way, which is a complete reversal of the values of the world as she knew it. While the *Magnificat* is lovely, it is extraordinarily powerful because it speaks of total trust in God, which often quite naturally leads to following an unfamiliar way. Within the child-self that is part of us all, there is perhaps nothing more precious than the fathomless capacity to trust.

Outside the city of Cairo, Egypt, on the edge of a high limestone hill, is a large slum where many thousands of garbage collectors live. It is an indescribably filthy area, with pigs walking all around, and the smell is almost unbearable in the desert heat. Years ago Father Samaan Ibrahim, a Coptic Orthodox priest, moved into this forsaken place to serve its people. Today the garbage collectors and their families worship in massive caves carved out of the rock hill, and they even have a school, a vocational training center, and a medical clinic. Astonishingly, every Thursday evening thirteen thousand people gather to worship in the large carved-out amphitheater.

Thinking about the revolutionary note in Mary's song about following Christ's new way, I am reminded of a worshiper I met during one of those Thursday evening gatherings, a young garbage collector's son named Yusuf. A number of years ago, at a Cairo construction site, an American executive lost his gold Rolex watch. Not long after, the young Yusuf, who was at that time an apprentice to his father, learning how best to collect garbage, found that gold watch. Because he was a follower of Christ, through Father Samaan's ministry among them, Yusuf felt led to find the watch's owner in order to return it. This was obviously a difficult decision, as that Rolex watch was worth more money than Yusuf would ever earn during his lifetime: more than twenty thousand dollars on the Cairo black market.

It took several months of looking and asking questions for Yusuf to discover the true owner of the Rolex watch. He learned that the owner was staying in a luxury apartment building in Cairo. As a poor garbage collector, wearing very dirty clothes, he would never have been let into this apartment *de luxe* through the lobby; he would have looked completely out of place. So Yusuf figured out a way to get in through a back exit door used for garbage removal. He climbed the stairs to the floor where the American executive was staying, and knocked on his door.

The American answered the door, somewhat astonished to see someone in the hallway dressed as shabbily as Yusuf. "You lost something?" Yusuf nervously blurted out in his minimal English. Several months had gone by since the man had lost his Rolex watch, so it didn't come to the man's mind. "Did you lose this watch?" Yusuf asked, as he took the watch out of the pocket in his dirty robe. When he saw his watch, the stunned American invited Yusuf into his apartment.

When they were sitting down, he asked, "Tell me, why you didn't keep it yourself?"

Yusuf replied, "Christ taught in the gospels to give to Caesar what is Caesar's and to God what is God's."

"But why didn't you take it and sell it?" the American persisted.

"It's not mine. It's not my right. I must be honest — it's not my watch. Christ said not to steal."

The American asked him, "Are you a Christian?"

"Yes," Yusuf replied.

Miraculously, that American, who described himself as an agnostic, renewed his faith in God because of this example of the revolutionary teaching of Christ being followed by that garbage collector's son.

He wrote in his diary, "I came back to God because of a poor Egyptian Christian garbage collector in Cairo." Just as the life of Yusuf the garbage collector, transformed by Christ's teaching, had its own transforming impact on the life of another, so Mary's song proclaims the transformative dimension of God's mercy that fills the hungry and gives strength to those who are without power in this world.

This Advent and Christmas, as we prepare ourselves for the celebration of the coming of Christ, we are all called to be children once again through this story of all stories. And the *Magnificat* reminds us that there dwells in the heart of each and every one of us a song, music that we alone know how to sing and play, about *believing* God, and *receiving* from God, and *trusting* in God beyond measure.

Ever since that Child was born, people have become enraptured by him, and in their enchantment they have become childlike in the best sense of the word. Countless numbers of different kinds of people have been caught up into his life in all sorts of ways. Untold numbers have found themselves healed and transformed by him in deep and private ways, so that they simply have no choice but to go on proclaiming what the Christmas narrative proclaims: that he is indeed the long expected one, the Christ. That he is our Wonderful Counselor, our Mighty God, the Everlasting Father, and the Prince of Peace. All these curious and foreboding terms that Christians continue to use are attempts to express in language one thing and one thing only: that dwelling in this Child is the power of God to bring light into our darkness and to make us whole. This Child yearns to give a new kind of life to anyone who turns to him, even to such as you and me. This is the treasure of which Mary sings, and which can be ours as well.

His Name is John by Daniel Bonnell

His Name is John

by Daniel Bonnell

In Luke 1:57–79 we read about the birth of John the Baptist. Zechariah, John's father, is finally able to speak to the family gathering, "His name is John," he proclaims in great joy. In this painting, called *His Name is John,* we see a symbolist painting that seeks to capture the joyful spirit of worship that filled that space and time. Zechariah presents John to the symbol of the heavenly Father in the sun. The sun directs its rays toward Mary, who in worship beholds the mystery of the Lion of Judah, her son.

The moon, which turns into a spiral jetty of water, is a symbol of John the Baptist being a reflection of the light, not the source of the light. Spiral jetties of water transform the darkness into light as death into life. Yet the most gripping element in the whole painting is a small red lamb, the crucified Christ. It is the heart of the painting, as all of life revolves around its sacrifice. The Holy Spirit of peace is seen etched out of a white cloud to balance the overall painting.

The Russian Jewish artist Marc Chagall was my mentor for this painting, along with the American Jewish painter Ben Shaw. Chagall painted romantic raptures of dreams; Shaw painted the drama of waiting in pain. Here I try to merge both of their visual attitudes into one painting.

Chapter Two

The Divine Synthesis

THE *BENEDICTUS, or*
SONG OF ZECHARIAH

When it was time for Elizabeth to have her baby, she gave birth to a son. Her neighbors and relatives heard that the Lord had shown her great mercy, and they shared her joy.

On the eighth day they came to circumcise the child, and they were going to name him after his father Zechariah, but his mother spoke up and said, "No! He is to be called John."

They said to her, "There is no one among your relatives who has that name."

Then they made signs to his father, to find out what he would like to name the child. He asked

for a writing tablet, and to everyone's
astonishment he wrote, "His name is John."
Immediately his mouth was opened and his
tongue was loosed, and he began to speak,
praising God. The neighbors were all filled
with awe, and throughout the hill country of
Judea people were talking about all these
things. Everyone who heard this wondered
about it, asking, "What then is this child going
to be?" For the Lord's hand was with him.

His father Zechariah was filled with the Holy
Spirit and prophesied:

"Praise be to the Lord, the God of Israel,
    because he has come
        and has redeemed his people.
He has raised up a horn of salvation for us
    in the house of his servant David
(as he said through his holy prophets
    of long ago),
salvation from our enemies
    and from the hand of all who hate us—
to show mercy to our fathers
    and to remember his holy covenant,
the oath he swore to our father Abraham:
    to rescue us from the hand of our
        enemies,
and to enable us to serve him without fear
    in holiness and righteousness before him
        all our days.

And you, my child, will be called a prophet
  of the Most High;
for you will go on before the Lord to
  prepare the way for him,
to give his people the knowledge of
  salvation
through the forgiveness of their sins,
  because of the tender mercy of our God,
by which the rising sun will come to us
  from heaven
to shine on those living in darkness
  and in the shadow of death,
to guide our feet into the path of peace."

(Luke 1:57–79)

It is in the spirit of rejoicing, due to the announce-ment of the forthcoming birth of the Christ child, that in this season of waiting and joy Luke gives us a second song, the Song of Zechariah, traditionally re-ferred to as the *Benedictus*. A song of great spiritual depth, the *Benedictus* is the song of thanksgiving that Zechariah sings when his speech returns to him after his son John (who came to be known as John the Baptist) is born. This song is his expression of grati-tude to God both for the fulfillment of his people's messianic hopes — Zechariah now understands the Messiah is coming — and also for giving him a child.

Essentially a hymn of adoration, *Benedictus* means "praise be." They are the first words in the Latin Vulgate translation of the Song of Zechariah. Over the centuries, the *Benedictus* has played a role of great importance in the worship of the church around the world. In some Western churches, such as Roman Catholic, Anglican, and Lutheran, the *Benedictus* is sung every day in the service of Morning Prayer. The Eastern Orthodox Church prescribes it to be sung daily as well.

Perhaps the primary reason for the popularity over the ages of the *Benedictus* is that it serves as a guide to enable us to see how God may be blessed, in the sense of being praised. Luke portrays the entire life of Christ in his gospel from the perspective of a blessing. He begins his story about Jesus with the priest Zechariah in the temple of Jerusalem, during the time for sacrifice, which is why in church tradition an ox, a sacrificial animal, became the symbol for Luke. However, he presents Zechariah as unable to pronounce the blessing on the people because he has been struck mute. Luke ends his narrative back in another liturgical setting, when Jesus, after the resurrection, leads his disciples out of the city and blesses them with uplifted hands. Luke writes his gospel account as the fulfillment of a blessing, a benediction; the unfinished worship service in the temple at the beginning is completed at the end. Luke brilliantly brings this narrative of blessing to life in his vivid writing style. An expert storyteller, he is able to paint a picture of each event in colorful detail—indeed, from the sixth century onward, tradition records that Luke was not just a medical doctor, but also a painter.

In order to understand and interpret Zechariah's song most fully, the song must first be seen through Zechariah's life and prayers, as it is integrally interwoven with them. Luke begins his story with these words: "In the time of Herod king of Judea there was a priest named Zechariah, who belonged to the priestly division of Abijah; his wife Elizabeth was also a descendant of Aaron." He gives the reader a time, a place, a set of characters; he lets us know the implied promise that something is coming, creating an atmosphere of great expectation. Luke beautifully and powerfully captures in words one of those unique moments in time. Every once in a while life can be eloquent. We go along from day to day not noticing very much, not really seeing or hearing, and then suddenly, when we least expect it, something speaks to us with such power that it catches us off guard, requiring us to listen. It is an experience that calls us by name and forces us to look where we hadn't had the heart to look before, and perhaps to hear something that for years we hadn't had the courage to hear.

The extraordinary thing about Zechariah was his faith. He is often portrayed in a negative cast, as one with little faith, someone who did not believe and therefore had his speech taken away from him. However, it is critical that he be seen in the light of his own personal life situation. He and his wife Elizabeth were both from priestly descent, from the line of Aaron. It was an honor to have a wife of priestly descent, as Zechariah himself was a priest. At that time there was no retirement age for priests, and Luke tells us that they were quite old, and still childless, something seen as disgraceful in the shame-based culture of the Middle East. In Jewish rabbinic law, failure to produce a child was grounds for divorce. And while not having a child was quite a negative stigma, not having a son was far more dishonorable.

Often "children" and "sons" are synonymous in a patriarchal society. When I lived in Tunisia, North Africa, a taxi driver once asked me if I had any children. I shared with him that I had a little girl (our son hadn't yet been born then). Astonishingly, he responded, "I asked you if you had any children?" He refused to count our daughter as of any significance, and was really asking if I had a son. Certainly, Zechariah and Elizabeth experienced a great deal of humiliation and most probably were shunned by some in the community. Many people at the time saw childlessness as a curse, and believed that someone in the family had probably committed some secret wrong. Yet through all of these challenges Zechariah and Elizabeth's hearts remained sensitive. Luke describes them as "upright," carrying no bitterness in spite of their discouragement over the years.

In addition to Zechariah's personal situation, one of his chief responsibilities as a priest was to assist the people in their knowledge of and communication with God. Zechariah lived at a time that has been referred to as the "silent years," a period between the Hebrew Scriptures and the New Testament when in effect God seemed silent to the Jewish people, for what they called "prophecy" had ended. Ever since returning from their Babylonian exile, for almost four hundred years, the Jewish people had experienced a faraway and distant God. Nevertheless, they still prayed for (even if barely) and still hoped (even if just) that their Christ, the Messiah, their Savior, would come. And Zechariah was one of the priests selected to lead the people in this hopeful prayer, even though he, like his people, heard and saw nothing of the Messiah himself. We are reminded of those haunting words from Shakespeare, "How like a winter hath my absence been from thee."

It was this type of winter, an absence from God, in which the Jews found themselves. T. S. Eliot's marvelous poem "East Coker" in his *Four Quartets* describes this paradoxically as "waiting without hope." Waiting for something indicates some level of hope that it will come. At the same time it seems like the Jewish people are waiting hopelessly. Eliot goes on to say that in this kind of waiting, darkness is the only light one knows, stillness the only dancing.

One day as they cast the lot to determine who would keep the incense burning in the most holy place of the temple, the lot fell on Zechariah. At that

time there were approximately twenty thousand
priests, far too many to serve all at the same time in
the temple. Therefore, since the time of King David,
the priests were divided up into twenty-four divisions
of approximately one thousand each. Zechariah was
of the division of Abijah. Each priest was responsible
for a week's service at the temple every six months,
which entailed teaching the Scriptures, directing worship, and maintaining the upkeep of the temple. The
division of Abijah was eighth on the roster. At the beginning of each week they drew lots (cast dice) as to
who would do what: the ultimate responsibility and
honor was to be selected to go into the most holy
place, and to refresh the supply of incense on the
altar, in order to keep it burning, before the morning
and evening sacrifice. As the smoke of the incense
rose from the altar, the people outside in the court-
yard joined in silent prayer. The smoke drifting upward symbolized their prayers ascending to God's
throne for the coming of the Messiah. And a priest
could be assigned this duty only once in a lifetime.

It is critical to understand that this is the most important moment of Zechariah's life. Clothed in white
robes, his head covered, shoes off, incense in hand,
facing east, he enters alone, the most holy place in the
temple. And there, while filling the incense and praying his greatest prayer, with reverence and even trepidation, an angel named Gabriel appears to him
between the altar of incense and the golden candle-

stick, and says to him, "Your prayer has been heard."
In fact, the angel's announcement has a double meaning: You will have a son, he tells Zechariah, and that
son will "make ready a people prepared for the Lord."
These two announcements are jointly pronounced.
They cannot be separated, for the angel's announce-
ment interweaves the Messiah's coming *and* the coming of a son for them as couple. In this double
entendre a "divine synthesis" is revealed. Old and
childless, Zechariah and Elizabeth are to receive a
son who fits into the larger purposes of God in their
nation: the coming of their Messiah.

The rite of offering incense usually took a very
short time, so Zechariah's delay in the most holy place
caused alarm; perhaps he had died, the people wor-
ried. However, when he eventually came out, he was
mute and therefore unable to communicate what had
happened. Everyone is confused, though Zechariah is
able to make signs clearly enough that they knew he
had seen a vision. Zechariah and Elizabeth then go
to the hills for five months, perhaps not only to get
away from the rumors flying around, but also to ponder what all this meant for them. In the sixth month,
Zechariah would have returned to Jerusalem to serve
again at the temple.

We next hear about Zechariah at his new son's circumcision ceremony, eight days after his birth. Tradition required the child to remain nameless until this
ceremony of giving the child to God. While potential

names were debated by relatives and friends, it was
traditionally the father's responsibility. However, due
to his inability to speak, his wife Elizabeth says the
child's name is to be John, not Zechariah, after his
father as would traditionally be the case. Surprised,
the people looked to the father, and Zechariah writes
his response on a tablet: "His name is John." This
grammatical tense indicates something extremely important had happened in Zechariah's life. He doesn't
write, "His name will be John," but he acknowledges
than in a sense the child is *already* John. Zechariah is
saying that he now finally understands what God is
doing through what we may term a "divine synthesis." The ultimate of dreams for their people was finally to take place and they, through the birth of this
miraculous son, were to be a part of it. Immediately
Zechariah's speech is restored and he bursts forth in
song, the *Benedictus*, becoming an eloquent witness to
a new era of the way God chooses to work. In this
song of Zechariah's, we get a glimpse of this divine
synthesis, the coming together of a single child who
both fulfilled his parent's most cherished hopes and
prepared the way for the coming of the long-awaited
Messiah.

The Merciful God of History

The first part of the *Benedictus* is about God working out the divine plan for the Messiah's coming, redeeming his people by fulfilling the promise of mercy made through the prophets and remembering "his holy covenant, the oath he swore to our father Abraham." As a priest of the Jewish people, Zechariah praises God for rescuing them from their enemies so that they might "serve him without fear in holiness and righteousness" for the rest of their days.

When Zechariah was praying inside the most holy place in the temple, it seems very unlikely that at such a moment he would have prayed for a private concern like reversing his childlessness state. Rather, he would have prayed, like all faithful Jews at that time, for the coming of the Messiah—it would have been foremost in his mind. Likewise, in the first part of his song he recalls hundreds of years of God's sovereign work in history, beginning with Abraham and moving through the prophets to his own day. The Hebrew Scriptures are a beautiful mosaic portraying God's involvement in the lives of the children of Israel. Regardless of the circumstances, God's plan remains clear for the Israelites throughout their history recorded in the Scriptures, regardless of the famines, the four hundred thirty years of captivity, the Exodus, the desert wanderings, the Babylonian exile, and throughout the "silent years" in which Zechariah finds himself and his people.

Zechariah is reminding us that God is a God of history. Perhaps this is why Luke introduces his "life of Christ" with such extraordinary detail, including the names of rulers and their respective territories. He is emphasizing that God is involved in history; that God is actively accomplishing his ultimate purposes in this world—past, present, and future. Throughout the Advent season, the church's lectionary readings focus on the *eschaton*—the last things, the second coming of Christ, the future. And this theme relates to the concept of the providence of God that can be seen throughout the Scriptures. Often referred to as "general providence," it connotes an element of "divine prearrangement" in the sometimes seemingly random events of human history.

This is certainly one of the greatest of divine mysteries. God isn't just the God of the universe, but also of the affairs of this world: within countries, governments, and popular movements. While Zechariah is singing specifically about the people of Israel and God's activity in their history, his words could make sense to any people or country. And if God is about divine ultimate purposes, it means God often moves in unrecognized events and processes. I recall the fascinating way Archbishop Desmond Tutu has recounted the history of the collapse of apartheid in South Africa. When seen retrospectively, he can observe how each event unfolded into another, eventually leading to the gradual desegregation of their peoples. More often than not, this is all mystery, as paradox seems to be God's *modus operandi*. It is as if history is both planned and unplanned at the same time. However one looks at it, Zechariah's song means that God is about his purposes everywhere, even in the present day Middle East. God is busy accomplishing his purposes in all places, regardless of whether they are visible or tangible to us.

I always enjoy hearing the well-known song that we used to sing in church school with the refrain, "He's got the whole world in his hands." With this understanding, we need never fear, no matter what global crises or world tragedies emerge, as God is always in the picture to accomplish divine purposes in spite of them; they are not obstacles to him. This truth provides us a profound confidence. We never need to ask "What is this world coming to?" or "Where is the world going?" Neither do we need to feel the complete responsibility of taking it all into our own hands.

Zechariah sings not only about God at work and in control of all things at all times, but he also praises an overwhelmingly comforting dimension of God. He sings about a God who has come to "show mercy." Throughout Luke's infancy narrative mercy is the prominent theme. Mercy is the determinant of God's purposes in history. All of God's actions are governed by this overriding dimension of mercy. This is the heart of the Jewish people's story as told in the Scriptures. Before the close of the Old Testament period, prior to the beginning of the "silent years," despite enduring one form of rebellion by the children of Israel after another, we see God's mercy prevailing. According the words of Jeremiah, God says, "The time is coming when I will make a new covenant with the house of Israel and with the house of Judah.... I will be their God, and they will be my people.... For I will forgive their wickedness and will remember their sins no more" (Jeremiah 31:31, 33–34).

In the early church's Christmas tradition, mercy is regarded as the gift of the Incarnation, with Christ's coming among us viewed essentially as the fullest demonstration of the mercy of God. The early nativity hymns of Ephrem the Syrian personify Christ as "mercy." Augustine of Hippo in North Africa used "mercy" virtually as another name for God. Interestingly, the first line of the Qur'an, the Muslim holy book, begins with the words, "In the Name of God [Allah], the Merciful and Compassionate."

All of this corresponds beautifully with Zechariah's agreement to name his son John, which is derived from *Johanan,* meaning "God is gracious." The first part of Zechariah's song reminds us that God is a God of history, who is busy accomplishing divine purposes, with mercy at the heart of them all.

The Tenderness of the God of History

The second part of Zechariah's song stands in sharp contrast to the first, as he turns to address his son John: "And you, my child...." Zechariah moves from singing about God's ultimate purposes in the world to affirming the truth of God's very personal activity in his own life. In a tender contrast, he personalizes the story to himself. He will have a son, and his son is going to play a key role in the greatest drama of all time. The angel Gabriel in effect said to him, "Your prayer for the Messiah is answered *and* you are to have a son who will prepare his way."

This is how God chooses to work, carrying out divine purposes through personal involvement in our lives. God goes about fulfilling eternal work in the world by meeting our individual needs. God's bigger plans are all interwoven with each of our own life journeys of faith, the "divine synthesis" of which Zechariah sings. This care over the life and activity of creation is often referred to as "special providence." It is what the apostle Paul is pointing toward when he writes to the church in Rome, "In all things God works for the good of those who love him" (Romans 8:28). Often in speaking of providence, one runs across the phrase "second causes," which are the or-

dinary forces and events of nature that God employs
to accomplish divine purposes.

It is difficult to understand why God let Zechariah
and Elizabeth experience so much emotional pain for
so long before bringing forth John's birth. However,
when it did happen, Zechariah saw more clearly after
his suffering than he could have otherwise; he could
see how all things come together in God's purposes.
Hence the second line of that church school children's
song: God not only has the whole world in his hands,
"He's got the little tiny baby in his hands." God's ultimate purposes are accomplished through personal
promises; the two are intricately linked.

The patriarch Joseph is a favorite of today's Middle Eastern Christians because of his important role
in Egypt, and he is an exceptional illustration of how
this great synthesis works. He went through incredible suffering: he was betrayed by his brothers and
sold into slavery in Egypt; his character was later de-
famed and he was held as a captive in prison for
years. However, through all the tragedy Joseph experienced, God worked through it to enable him to
play the key role necessary to rescue his people, the
Israelites, during a time of great famine. His life challenges enabled him to take part in God's bigger purposes, so that he could finally say these remarkable
words to his brothers who had sold him many years
before into slavery: "Do not be distressed and do not
be angry with yourselves for selling me here, because

it was to save lives that God sent me ahead of
you.... God sent me ahead of you...to save your
lives by a great deliverance. So then, it was not you
who sent me here, but God" (Genesis 45:5–8).

As children of God we are part of God's ultimate
purposes wherever we are. It is a beautiful thing
when we as individuals, like Joseph and Zechariah,
catch a glimpse of ourselves in the divine picture, seeing our life experiences as part of God's plan. This
perspective is often encountered when reading the
autobiographical accounts of those who have undergone great suffering, such as Nelson Mandela, who
endured the struggles of apartheid and imprisonment;
Elie Wiesel, who survived the Holocaust; and
Alexander Solzhenitsyn, who withstood Stalin's
Gulag and exile. Knowing we are involved in God's
purposes enables us to see the deeper meaning of life's
challenges, nurturing a more holistic perspective.

This experience can be likened to finding yourself
in a large group photograph taken many years ago.
At first, identifying yourself can be difficult. However, when you do locate your face, the memories
come back in full force. Seeing the person sitting next
to you, and the one three rows in front, you realize
how interconnected all our lives were. Every one of
us is intricately related to the working out of God's
ultimate purposes. And catching an awareness of how
our lives are involved in God's bigger purposes can

provide tremendous meaning and hope in the midst of
the hardships life presents.

Zechariah sings that the greatest surprise for him
was to see that he was playing a part in the ongoing
history of God's redemptive work in the world. In so
doing, he gives us encouragement as to the *why* and
how of all this: it is all "because of the tender mercy of
our God." Again he focuses on the mercy of God, yet
now he personalizes this trait of God, referring to it as
"tender." Prior to Zechariah's song, Luke too placed
the event of John's birth firmly in this context, writing of Elizabeth that "the Lord had shown her great
mercy." And in Zechariah's song, mercy continues as
the foundation of God's activity in the world—not
just to the people of Israel, but also specifically to
Zechariah and his wife, Elizabeth. God chose to ful-
fill the divine ultimate purpose—sending the Messiah—by providing a discouraged couple the greatest
encouragement ever. In doing so, our Creator is ex-
emplifying the preeminent divine character traits of
mercy and compassion.

The Christ Child is in effect an "Ambassador of
Mercy" from "God the Merciful and Compassionate."
Perhaps this is the most accurate description of
Christ's life and purpose. Hence we have that won-
derful Latin phrase known in church worship as the
Kyrie eleison, taken from the many individuals who
came to Christ, falling at his feet in desperation, say-
ing, "Lord, have mercy." I once saw a stirring paint-

ing by the mid-nineteenth-century Austrian painter
Gabriel C. Max titled *Healing the Sick*. It portrays a
mother bringing her sick, helpless, and feverish child
to Jesus. As she stands in front of Jesus, the mother's
face holds a look of expectancy as she ponders the
tender face of Jesus. While the healing hadn't yet
taken place, the artist was able to capture the healing
nature of Jesus in such a way that one can almost
"see" the healing already, as Christ's face is one of
mercy personified.

I am reminded of that beautiful phrase of Augustine of Hippo when, referring to a man falling into a
river, he writes, "The mercy of God may be found between the bridge and the stream." Because of God's
heart of mercy, God comes to our aid over and over
again, just as he did for Zechariah. At the same time,
it is these merciful actions that are interwoven with
the divine purposes for our world. Zechariah sings a
song that has now been sung for almost two thousand
years, giving thanks for the gift of perceiving the divine synthesis of God. It is this divine synthesis that
is the wild and joy-filled proclamation of Advent and
Christmas.

God's ultimate purposes for the world are carried
out by working through a baby and childless parents:
through the strong and the weak, the expected and
unexpected, the perfectly natural and the supernatu-
ral—and in you and me. All are mysteriously con-
nected to God's bigger agenda. In this regard, the first

words of Zechariah's *Benedictus*, "Praise be to God,"
are the most appropriate of all. May we each glimpse
this divine synthesis in our lives this holy season.

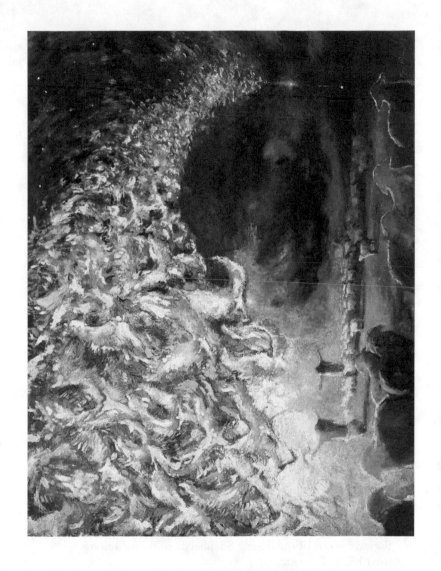

The Seeing Shepherds by Daniel Bonnell

The Seeing Shepherds

by Daniel Bonnell

In Luke 2:8–20 we read of the shepherds who came face to face with an angel who proclaimed, "Do not be afraid. I bring you good news of great joy that will be for all the people. Today in the town of David a Savior has been born to you; he is Christ the Lord." Then we read that a great company of angels appeared, praising God and singing.

God always does things upside down, backwards to the front and reverse to forward. The angels appear to the humble blue-collar workers, the shepherds. Jesus is not born in a fancy birthing center but a smelly cave dwelling, in an animal stall. Mary's baby shower was quite different as well: three strangers with gifts that were anything but a month's supply of diapers.

In *The Seeing Shepherds*, the night sky is filled with color that is unknown to the human eye. What color is made when a host of angels beat their wings? What does a host of angels even begin to look like? The angels proceed directly from the point of the humble shepherds to surround the manger many miles away. The English painter J.M. William Turner would swoon viewers with a myriad of color. In the same manner, I hope to rapture my viewers into the painting as if they were one of the Seeing Shepherds standing among their herd of sheep.

Chapter Three

Seeing with the Eyes of Angels

And there were shepherds living out in the fields nearby, keeping watch over their flocks at night. An angel of the Lord appeared to them, and the glory of the Lord shone around them, and they were terrified. But the angel said to them, "Do not be afraid. I bring you good news of great joy that will be for all the people. Today in the town of David a Savior has been born to you; he is Christ the Lord.

This will be a sign to you: You will find a baby wrapped in cloths and lying in a manger."

Suddenly a great company of the heavenly host appeared with the angel, praising God and saying,

> "Glory to God in the highest,
>   and on earth peace to men on
>   whom his favor rests."

When the angels had left them and gone into heaven, the shepherds said to one another, "Let's go to Bethlehem and see this thing that has happened, which the Lord has told us about."

So they hurried off and found Mary and Joseph, and the baby, who was lying in the manger. When they had seen him, they spread the word concerning what had been told them about this child, and all who heard it were amazed at what the shepherds said to them. But Mary treasured up all these things and pondered them in her heart. The shepherds returned, glorifying and praising God for all the things they had heard and seen, which were just as they had been told.

(Luke 2:8–20)

Glory is not a word we use much in our contemporary vocabulary. My father was a minister and I never remember him swearing. However, he selected other words as substitutes. One of his most common was the word "Glory." Anytime he was upset, frustrated, or physically in pain, we would hear the word "Glory" ring out throughout the house.

Luke is the gospel writer who shares with us that marvelous encounter of the angels visiting the shepherds at night and singing, "Glory to God in the highest, and on earth peace to men on whom his favor rests." Glory is certainly the theme of this nativity experience of the shepherds. This theme is most magnificently captured by Rembrandt in an etching and engraving he did of this scene. There, in the middle of a Judean night, the darkness was shattered, as if the light were a hundred suns; the night sky came alive with the radiance of angels, in full view of the shepherds tending to their flocks in the darkness. What had been a silent night for those shepherds was suddenly resounding with the beating of thousands and thousands of the bright wings of angels, and also sound of their voices, like trumpets, singing a hymn of praise.

An angel tells the startled shepherds not to fear, for his message is full of joy: "a Savior has been born to you." And suddenly the angel is joined by thousands more, all praising God and saying, "Glory to God in the highest, and on earth peace." The universe seems to provide a stage, with Jesus as the drama. Lord Byron, the great English poet of the early 1800s, spent a good bit of time in the Middle East, an experience that provided material for his later works. Upon his return to England, he wrote *The Giaour*, which includes these wonderful lines:

> Yes, love indeed is light from heaven;
>   A spark of that immortal fire
> With angels shared, by Allah given,
>   To lift from earth our low desire.

One of the reasons that this scene is so powerful is that Luke used various creative mediums when writing his gospel. An outstanding storyteller who knew how to use words to "paint the scenes" of Jesus' life in vivid detail, Luke describes the angelic surprise appearance to the shepherds of Bethlehem so beautifully that it has become the most familiar scene in all the florid history of religious art, with its visual nature etched in our memories. And in the same portrait Luke gives us the most popular of the songs sung in honor of the Christ Child's birth, the *Gloria*, the song of the angels to the shepherds.

The Advent and Christmas seasons remind us that singing is an integral part of our own celebration. Today this is nowhere more evident than on Christmas Eve just outside the eastern part of Bethlehem, when carols are sung at a twilight service held on the Shepherds' Fields. It is certainly cold standing out at night on those fields during the month of December; one can imagine the suffering endured during the great winter snowfall of 1910–11, when thousands of sheep died because the snow covered the ground for weeks. Today these Shepherds' Fields are fenced off by low stone walls and rows of silver-green olive trees. Luke's shepherds, whose lives were dramatically changed by the angel's song that cold winter night, may have lived in the little herdsmen's village of Beit Sahur, just below Bethlehem. Shepherding is perhaps the least changed occupation in Palestine over the last two thousand years. Each time I have visited Bethlehem and its surroundings, I have seen shepherds out in those fields, all bundled up to keep warm, as they watch over their sheep.

The Song of the Angels has great historical significance and contemporary meaning for us. *Gloria in excelsis,* the title taken from the first line in the Latin Vulgate of this canticle, means "Glory to God in the highest." This angelic utterance has become one of the most sacred texts of Christian liturgy. The *Gloria* has long been a hymn of praise in Christian worship, sung by the whole congregation in one form or another since before the fourth century, when it was said during Morning Prayer by the Greek church. In the sixth century it was used exclusively for papal masses, since it was viewed as the most important of the canticles. The *Gloria* went on to be incorporated into countless medieval hymns and carols. Down

through the years, composers have put it to score untold times, from Johann Sebastian Bach to Antonio
Vivaldi. Today, the *Gloria* is sung in many churches
on all feast days and Sundays, except during Advent
and Lent.

Certainly, part of the attraction to the *Gloria* over
the centuries has to do with the fact that it is indeed
a song of the angels. And angels played a most important role in the Christmas story, visiting significant characters like Joseph and Mary, Zechariah and
the shepherds. The word "angel" simply means "messenger." In the Christmas story they are God's messengers, representing God to the people. In other
words, they give to us a further glimpse of who God
is and what God intends to do.

This is why the usual reaction to angels in the
Christmas story includes an element of fear. Hence
the first words of the angel to shepherds standing in
the fields were, "Do not be afraid." The angel went
on to say that the message he was bringing from God
was "good news of great joy"—not bad news of impending disaster. Indeed, many Jewish people at that
time believed that the appearance of spirits during the
night foreshadowed disaster, so the angel immediately
reassures the shepherds that nothing could be further
from the truth.

The Goodness of God

What was this message that the angels were bringing from God all about? "Glory to God in the highest!" they sing. The word "glory" in Hebrew comes from a root word that means "weighty," indicating that their message was of tremendous importance. "Glory" was a word used by the Jews at that time as an attempt to describe the very nature of God. Throughout the Scriptures "glory" largely refers to the "display of God's character," implying a disclosure by God of who God is: an expression of God's active presence. Therefore, when the angels sing the *Gloria,* they are saying that Christ's birth is ultimately about revealing God's character, demonstrating the very heart of the Divine.

The angels sing, "Glory to God in the highest heaven, and on earth peace among those whom he favors!" (NRSV). Other translations read "peace, goodwill to all," or as William Barclay so beautifully paraphrased, "peace to those whose welfare he ever seeks." The angels are singing that Christ's birth is fundamentally about the goodwill of God, meaning divine pleasure — God's favor toward us, God's grace among us.

Jesus embodied a divine affirmation: an affirmation that God embraces us all. The core message of Christmas, of Christ's birth, what we call the Incarnation, is that God is all about being *for us*. This affirmation stands against a commonly held view still today that God is a God of punishment and reprimand, a God who looks down more in anger and displeasure than in love.

And it must be said that there are many passages in the Hebrew Scriptures that would seem to uphold such a mistaken view of God, for the experience of suffering by the Jewish people often led them to believe that God was punishing them for their sins. Yet in the same Scriptures there are also many moments when the loving nature of God was glimpsed and understood. When Moses, standing on Mount Sinai in Egypt, asked to see God's "glory," for example, the Lord replied, "I will cause all my *goodness* to pass in front of you" (Exodus 33:19). In other words, "the glory of God," meaning the "character of God," is fundamentally total goodness: God's deepest desire is goodwill toward us, his creation.

Referring to all this, C. S. Lewis writes in his sermon *The Weight of Glory* that we are "half-hearted creatures" who do not realize that "infinite joy" is being offered to us. We are like a "child who wants to go on making mud pies in a slum because he cannot imagine what is meant by the offer of a holiday at the sea. We are far too easily pleased." Lewis continues that the "promise of glory" is the incredible promise that we "shall find approval, shall please God.... To be loved by God, not merely pitied, but delighted in as an artist delights in his work... —it seems impossible, a weight or burden of glory which our thoughts can hardly sustain. But so it is."[7]

Salaam for All

After praising God's glory the angels go on to sing of peace on earth, emphasizing that God's desire for all people is peace. The heart of God, demonstrated in the giving of Christ, is that we all experience God's peace, what is called in Hebrew *shalom* and in Arabic *salaam*. *Shalom* does not primarily mean the cessation of conflict, but rather the experience of "complete wholeness." It is a word that tells us that God's deepest desire, embodying the heart of God, is to look after our total welfare. Throughout the Arab world the standard first greeting is *Salaam aleikuum,* a beautiful phrase that simply means "God's peace be upon you," but is widely understood as bestowing on the other God's blessing.

The angel's pronouncement of peace to all stands in contrast to the peace offered at that time by the Roman emperor, a peace referred to as the *Pax Ro-*

mana. The Roman peace was imposed and kept by harsh military rule and required the submission of conquered peoples; here, the shepherds were being offered the peace of God.

The nature of God's peace can also be seen in Johann Sebastian Bach's well-known sacred cantata titled *Gloria in Excelsis,* which was composed during the five-month mourning period following the death of his dear wife, Maria Barbara Bach, in 1720. Obviously, God met him in an intimate and extraordinary way during his time of pain and grief. We live in a world that is made up of hurting people, and God is in the business of healing, forgiving, restoring, giving new beginnings: making people whole. I recall the words of Sadhu Sundar Singh, the Indian Sikh follower of Christ, when Europeans asked him about the evolutionary notion of the survival of the fittest: "The fit will survive of themselves," he responded. "But in my experience, what I have seen is the survival of the unfit. And that is where God's glory comes in."[8]

During the twenty centuries since the Christ Child was born, countless people have been transformed by their relationship with him, seeing in him the power of God to bring light into our darkness, and to give us a new kind of life. I am reminded of a wonderful line by George Herbert, the seventeenth-century Anglican priest and poet, in his poem *An Offering*: "In Christ two natures met to be thy cure."

The angel's message to the shepherds was that "A Savior has been born"; a very special deliverer had come to them. We needed to be rescued from another dimension. So at Christmas we are reminded that God enters our world to bring salvation and wholeness. Or, as Simone Weil, the late French Jewish writer, expressed it so well, "God is longing to come down to those in affliction." And further, the angels tell us this good news of peace, this promised wholeness, this goodwill of God toward us, is "for all the people."

The message of the angels is that God's love, demonstrated by the sending of the Christ Child, was for *all* people, not just for the Jews or the "religious," as it was so often believed then. Luke continues throughout his gospel to emphasize that God's love is for all equally, putting great emphasis on Jesus' loving treatment of the poor, of women, the gentiles (non-Jews), and those considered "dishonorable" or "disreputable" in that society.

In Luke's nativity story this all-encompassing love is symbolized by the fact that the Christ Child's first visitors weren't of high status; they weren't powerful, religious, or wealthy. They were common laborers, shepherds to whom God had spoken in the middle of the night. At that time, shepherds were considered spiritually and religiously unclean, as they weren't able to keep all the religious ceremonial laws due to their occupation, so they were despised and not even allowed into the temple. Yet they are the first to be told of Christ's birth. It is a wonderful paradox, reflective of God's love for all. I love Queen Lucy's magnificent line in *The Last Battle* of the C. S. Lewis's *Chronicles of Narnia*: "In our world too, a stable once had something inside it that was bigger than our whole world."[9]

As a result of the birth of the Christ Child, we understand that any and every dimension of life can become an arena of God's extraordinary saving activity. This is why Christians celebrate Christmas as the single greatest moment in all of human history, as a character in C. S. Lewis's novel *Perelandra* says, "What had happened on Earth when [God] was born a man at Bethlehem had altered the universe forever."[10] Not only did God come to us in Jesus to deliver us, God also came to share our lives, and all that life brings to us, the good and the bad, in a way that simply staggers the human imagination.

When Matthew, in writing his account of Christ's birth, searched for a way to distill the essence of that first Christmas, he reached back seven hundred years to borrow a single verse from the book of Isaiah, and captured its truth in a single Hebrew word. Matthew first quotes from Isaiah: "The virgin will be with child and will give birth to a son, and they will call him *Immanuel*"—a Hebrew word which Matthew then translates for his readers, saying, "which means, 'God with us.'" By quoting this verse from Isaiah in his nativity story Matthew thus tells us that "God with us" is not just a translation of a Hebrew word, but a translation of the display of the loving heart of God. In the birth of this Child we see that God does not abandon us, Matthew affirms, but instead is *Immanuel*—one with us, so that we may experience God's heart for us fully.

The "good news of great joy" of which the angels sang is that God is not aloof or remote. In that single word, Immanuel, resides the essence of what Christians believe happened at the birth of Jesus. In a divine descent, God entered our world to embrace and show us pure love. Therefore, regardless of whether we feel God's presence or not, God is near. We don't climb our way to heaven or to God, but rather God comes down to us, moving among and within us, making our ordinary lives extraordinary by his presence. My own favorite Christmas verse, filled with depth of imagery and beautiful cadence, comes from the deuterocanonical book The Wisdom of Solomon: "When all things lay in peace and silence, and night was in the midst of her swift course, God's Almighty Word leapt down from Heaven, out of His Royal Throne" (18:14–15, KJV).

Today it is commonly rumored that a popular king in one of the Arab countries often "disappears" and walks incognito among his people. Asked by his security detail and members of his parliament not to do so, out of concern for his safety, he responds, "How do you expect me to properly assist my people unless I know how they live?"

A friend working in the challenging circumstances of Baghdad sent me a few heart-wrenching poems he had written during a period of great disillusionment. He was experiencing great internal turmoil due to the tragic loss of life there. One of his poems was titled "Oh F**K." In the poem he says that what he means by that expletive is "Oh God, help us!" A few weeks later he sent me another poem. This time he titled his poem, "Jesus is in Baghdad," as he had begun to see God as present and at work there in the midst of the chaos and tragedy.

There are in other faiths moving foreshadowings of the Incarnation, perhaps most clearly in Buddhism. Their ancient "pre-New Testament era" stories tell of great Buddhist figures whose love for others made them decide to postpone indefinitely their entrance into Nirvana in order to return again and again into the world of suffering until the last person was "enlightened." Surely in these stories we hear echoes of our own belief in a God who sent his only Son into a suffering world in order to save it.

The Christmas story is about God's commitment to us. Christmas is not our show, it is God's. Christmas is a divine initiative, when God establishes a tangible relationship of love which Jesus represents. The secret to understanding the angels' song, and therefore really the secret of Christmas, is that it isn't about *giving* to God, but rather it is about *receiving* God most fully into our lives. The only one giving in this story is God. We have only to receive this holy miracle that breaks into the night, even in the darkest nights of our lives. God is the central character of this Christmas story, and therefore in all our stories.

Luke's account of this angelic utterance ends with the reaction of the shepherds. At first, they probably stood in amazement, asking themselves, "What next?" Jim Bishop's bestselling book *The Day Christ Was Born* has a humorous section where the shepherds, after the angels left, are discussing what they should do. After they decide to go to Bethlehem to see this Christ Child whom they had just been told about, one of them asks, "You are sure that this is not the work of some evil Egyptian magician who would steal our flocks [while we are away]?"

Yet they did choose to take the short journey to the stable, and after seeing the Child in the manger just as they had been promised, and spreading the word to all who would listen, they return to their fields praising and glorifying God, probably singing the same *Gloria* they had just heard from the angels. The shepherds' impulse to sing emerged from the realization that God was completely *for them*, in the deepest dimension. All of this echoes what Martin Luther, the great church reformer, preached in a sermon on the birth of Jesus, almost five hundred years ago: "Of what benefit would it be to me if Jesus would have been born a thousand times and it would have been sung daily in my ears that Jesus Christ was born, but that I was never to hear that Jesus Christ was born for me?"

When I was working in Russia in the early 1990s, on a project that involved visiting orphanages, I remember hearing about an experience of two Americans at the time who were working with the Russian Department of Education and teaching in a large orphanage. During the Christmas season they shared with the children at the orphanage the story of Christ's birth: about Mary and Joseph arriving in Bethlehem but finding no room in the inn, and having to go to a stable, where the baby Jesus was born and placed in a manger.

After completing the story, they gave each child three small pieces of cardboard to make a crude manger, and a small paper square. Following the instructions, the children tore their papers and carefully laid strips in their manger for straw. Small squares of flannel, cut from a worn-out nightgown, were used for the baby's blanket. A doll-like baby was cut from tan felt the Americans had brought from the United States.

The American teachers walked among the children, who were busy assembling their mangers, to see if they needed any help. All went well until they got to one table where little Misha sat. He was about six years old and had finished his project. Looking at the little boy's manger, they were surprised to see not one, but two babies in the manger. Calling the translator over, they asked the little boy why there were two babies in the manger. Looking at his completed manger scene, the child began to repeat the story very seriously, relating the happenings quite accurately, until he came to the part where Mary put the baby Jesus in the manger. Then Misha started to ad-lib.

He made up his own ending to the story, as he said, "And when Maria laid the baby in the manger, Jesus looked at me and asked me if I had a place to stay. I told him I have no mother and I have no father, so I don't have any place to stay. Then Jesus told me I could stay with him. But I told him I couldn't, because I didn't have a gift to give him like everybody else did. But I wanted to stay with Jesus so much, so I thought about what I had that maybe I could use for a gift. I thought maybe if I kept him warm, that would be a good gift. So I asked Jesus, 'If I keep you warm, will that be a good enough gift?' And Jesus told me, 'If you keep me warm, that will be the best gift anybody ever gave me.' So I got into the manger...."

As we prepare during Advent for our response to God this Christmas, perhaps "keeping Jesus warm," in our own lives and hearts, is what it is really all about.

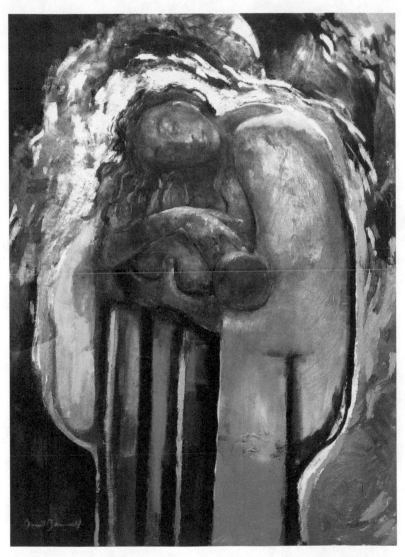

A Sword Shall Pierce Your Heart by Daniel Bonnell

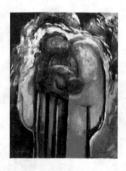

A Sword Shall Pierce Your Heart

by Daniel Bonnell

In Luke 2:25–35 we read of a devout Jewish elder in
Jerusalem who has his lifelong wish fulfilled: to behold
the Christ with his own eyes before dying. Simeon was
his name. Upon holding the infant Christ he proclaims
over the child various prophetic directives, only to end
by looking Mary in the eye and declaring, "And a sword
will pierce your own soul too."

In this painting, *A Sword Shall Pierce Your Heart,* I have
sought a visual paradox, that of suffering and elation. It
is the essential element of every disciple of Jesus. We are
to suffer his sufferings by carrying his cross for others.
Without the crucifixion, there is no resurrection.

Lastly, Mary is in bliss, swooned in being a mother. The
presence of the Father embraces Mary and her son with
a gold aura. Hers is the face of an angel, a mother, a new
bride.

Chapter Four

A Released Life

When the time of their purification according
to the Law of Moses had been completed,
Joseph and Mary took him to Jerusalem to
present him to the Lord (as it is written in the
Law of the Lord, "Every firstborn male is to be
consecrated to the Lord"), and to offer a
sacrifice in keeping with what is said in the
Law of the Lord: "a pair of doves or two young
pigeons."

Now there was a man in Jerusalem called
Simeon, who was righteous and devout. He
was waiting for the consolation of Israel, and
the Holy Spirit was upon him. It had been

revealed to him by the Holy Spirit that he would not die before he had seen the Lord's Christ. Moved by the Spirit, he went into the temple courts. When the parents brought in the child Jesus to do for him what the custom of the Law required, Simeon took him in his arms and praised God, saying:

"Sovereign Lord, as you have promised,
    you now dismiss your servant in peace.
For my eyes have seen your salvation,
    which you have prepared in the sight
    of all people,
a light for revelation to the Gentiles
    and for glory to your people Israel."

The child's father and mother marveled at what was said about him. Then Simeon blessed them and said to Mary, his mother: "This child is destined to cause the falling and rising of many in Israel, and to be a sign that will be spoken against, so that the thoughts of many hearts will be revealed. And a sword will pierce your own soul too."

(Luke 2:22–35)

The final Advent song Luke shares with us in his gospel account is perhaps the most profound. It is none other than that ancient canticle sung by a devout old man named Simeon in the temple when the baby Jesus was put into his arms. The church has held these four short verses close to its heart throughout the centuries ever since, using them liturgically from very early times. Augustine of Hippo, in the fourth century, would have sung this song in his evening prayers. Today in the rites of the Eastern Church, such as the historic churches of the Middle East, it is said at the evening service of Vespers. And in the Roman, Anglican, and other Western liturgies, like Mary's *Magnificat* it is said or sung at Evening Prayer or Compline. In the church's lectionary, the gospel story of Simeon is read on the festival of the Feast of the Presentation of our Lord in the Temple, known traditionally as Candlemas and celebrated on the fortieth day after Christmas. The Song of Simeon has been traditionally called the *Nunc Dimittis*, a title taken from the first words in the Vulgate Latin translation: *Nunc dimittis servum tuum, domine* — "Lord, now let your servant depart in peace."

The religious and liturgical events that provided the setting for this song were the traditional Jewish ceremonies that followed a baby's birth. Though they aren't clearly defined by Luke, who was not a Jew himself, three key Jewish ceremonies were taking place in the life of Mary, Joseph, and Jesus. The first ceremony was the Circumcision, which took place on the eighth day after birth. This was the time when the baby was named. It was considered such a sacred event that it could even be done on the Sabbath.

The second ceremony was the Redemption of the Firstborn, where the baby was presented to God one month after birth. This ceremony entailed the "buying back" or "redeeming" of the child from God through an offering. This symbolic action was an acknowledgment that the child belonged to God, and the parents were required to pay five shekels. Incidentally, according to Jewish law, this could only be done when the child was free of any physical deformation.

The third religious ceremony following a baby's birth was for the Purification of the Mother. This ceremony took place forty days after the birth of a son, or eighty days after a daughter. Prior to this event, the mother was considered ceremonially unclean and wasn't permitted to enter the temple. At the end of the "unclean period," the parents were to bring a lamb for a burnt offering and a dove or pigeon for a sin offering. If the lamb was too expensive for the parents' economic status, they were permitted to bring a second dove or pigeon, and this was most probably the case with Mary and Joseph.

It is for this third ceremony that they were at the temple and encountered Simeon in the temple courts. At this time the temple was approaching completion,

standing as a gleaming white jewel wedged into the
northeastern corner of the city, and to all pious Jews
this temple was the very center of the world. The
sprawling enclave was rimmed with a labyrinth of
colonnaded porticoes and gates. It was here, as Mary
and Joseph with their baby stood in the Court of the
Women, that an old man named Simeon, among the
most pious of all, came up to them. After taking the
baby in his arms, he sings a song that is like Hebrew
poetry, filled with scriptural language that closely
paralleled the words found in the book of Isaiah.

Who was Simeon? He is often written about in literature, and is frequently referred to in the poetry of
the Middle Ages. Artists throughout history have
never tired of trying to catch the sacred fire in
Simeon's eyes as he sings his song. Perhaps the most
striking effort is by the Dutch artist Rembrandt, who
painted this scene four times during his lifetime.
Simeon is usually presumed to be a priest since it is in
the temple that he presents himself and takes the baby
in his arms, which could perhaps be seen as a priestly
function. He is also often thought to be elderly, as we
are told that he waited so long for the arrival of the
Messiah. Augustine, while preaching in Carthage in
North Africa in the early fifth century, referred to
Simeon as "aged" and "long-lived." Furthermore, together with Simeon we are introduced to Anna, a
woman we are told is eighty-four years old.

It is a marvelous scene, with all the depth and
mystery one could ever hope for. We can almost feel
the chemistry of the moment as this old, gentle,
saintly, bent-over man takes this baby boy into his
arms and blesses him. And in so doing not only is the
baby boy blessed, but so also is the old saint. Simeon
clearly experiences something wonderful. It is a moment of grace in that great temple, when the child
Messiah is laid right into his arms and into his heart.
In response, he sings a song that has never stopped
being sung throughout Christendom.

Released to Live in the Present Moment

The *Nunc Dimittis* is ultimately a song about realizing
personal inner tranquility and restfulness — as we see
a spiritual calm brought to Simeon's life. This is why
it has been traditionally used during Evening Prayer
services, as the day closes for the night's rest. During
the season of Lent our church in Cairo has a midweek
contemplative service of Compline. For those who
come, it provides a spiritual calm in the midst of the
noise, chaos, dirt, and endless intensity of a city of
twenty-two million people. After this occasion, or
rather due to it, an internal peacefulness filled Simeon

as never before, thereby becoming for us a marvelous lesson in peaceful living.

Simeon sings, "Sovereign Lord, as you have promised, you now dismiss your servant in peace. For my eyes have seen your salvation." I love the way the writer Eugene Peterson paraphrases this line in *The Message*: "God, you can now release your servant; release me in peace as you promised. With my own eyes I've seen your salvation." The entire song is sung with the language of freedom. In the original Greek text, it has the connotation of releasing a slave. Simeon is describing his own experience as one of being released. In the song the word "now" is of utmost importance, emphasizing that an experience of profound liberation happened to him at that moment in time upon seeing the Christ Child.

Simeon's song is his way of describing how he was finally "released" truly to *live*. Many biblical commentators have interpreted his song as meaning he was at last free to die, presumably due to his old age after all those years of waiting to see the Messiah. However, the heart of Simeon's verse is that he was released into freedom, enabled to experience the gift of life anew. Essentially, Simeon now understood what it meant to be at peace with himself, because of what he "saw" in the temple.

What did he see? All he saw was a child, a little baby. However, this is profoundly symbolic; a baby, a new life, gives to an old one a new kind of life. There is a sense that a baby comes fresh from God, and is a part of God that we can hold. What Simeon saw made all the difference, providing this new sense of release to enter a new existence.

This sort of freedom is uniquely illustrated in words written from prison by Dietrich Bonhoeffer, the famous German Lutheran pastor and theologian. Imprisoned during the Advent season of 1943, toward the very end of World War II, for conspiring to overthrow Hitler, he wrote his fiancée these words: "A prison cell, in which one waits, hopes, does various unessential things, and is completely dependent on the fact that the door of freedom has to be opened *from the outside*, is not a bad picture of Advent."[11] God, through this Christ Child, has opened the "prison door" for Simeon, providing for him what the civil rights movement called "a way out of no way."

What exactly did this aged saint *see* when he sang, "For my eyes have *seen* your salvation"? I love the second painting Rembrandt did of this scene in 1631. The artist places the emphasis on Simeon with his typical *chiaroscuro*, the light shining right on his face and eyes. And Simeon, rather than looking at the child he is holding, is gazing up at God, with the baby's head slightly turned, his eyes watching Simeon's upward gaze. It is as if they are seeing beyond to something else. William Blake, the seventeenth-century English poet and artist, wrote in his poem "The Everlasting Gospel" of seeing things through or beyond their surface, as is happening in Rembrandt's painting.

> This life's dim windows of the soul
> Distorts the heavens from pole to pole
> And leads you to believe a lie
> When you see with, not through, the eye.

Blake is referring not just to seeing with the eyes, but to seeing the truth behind what is physically seen.

In Rembrandt's second painting of this scene it almost seems that Simeon and the Christ Child are looking up because they have heard a voice. If this is true, perhaps the more accurate question is, What did Simeon *hear* that so changed him? Interestingly, Simeon's name means "one who hears."

Whether by seeing or hearing, the best word to describe Simeon's experience here is almost certainly "revelation." A revelation is something like the clarity you experience when you have recovered from fainting: it isn't that the truth about something is coming out of nowhere and has never been there before, but rather that the truth is coming into focus as never before. What Simeon experienced is an illumination into his own experience and life, as well as a vision into new vistas on God's character. Whatever he saw (or heard), whatever was revealed to him at that moment, released him to a new understanding, experience, and dimension of living at peace, and of being at rest.

Simeon sings, "Lord, you now dismiss your servant in peace. For my eyes have seen your salvation."
As Simeon's song continues it appears that what he
saw, and what was revealed to him, was a fresh and
even wholly other perspective on God. In this regard,
it is helpful to recognize what sort of a man Simeon
was. We are told by Luke that he was a "righteous
and devout" man. The word "devout" implies that he
was cautious or extremely careful, referring to the religious laws and duties. Simeon may have been one
of what were called the Hasidim, those who were
conservative, strict in their worship, and who kept all
the religious law. Their reason for living in this way
was that their entire existence was devoted to one
thing: looking for, as it says of Simeon in Luke's
gospel, the "consolation of Israel," a phrase used to
signify the coming of the Messiah of the Jewish people. Therefore, his whole life was one of waiting.
Simeon's one purpose and focus was on the coming of
the Jewish Savior. Consequently, the Hasidim were
highly nationalistic. They were also known as the
"Quiet of the Land," for they were in constant prayer
and watchfulness, patiently on the "lookout" for the
Messiah. The Hasidim had waited for centuries. Now
they found themselves and their people under the
reign of gentile Romans, so it didn't look like the Messiah would be coming any time soon.

In addition, we must add to Simeon's already con-
suming purpose for living what had been revealed to

him by God's Spirit: he would not die before he had
seen the Messiah. With every passing year, his time
was running out. Simeon's very existence was for future possibilities. Obviously, he must have been driven
by this intensity of purpose. How could he have lived
in the present, when he lived for one future event? As
his life was slipping from him, approaching its end, we
can almost feel the burden of living with the restless-
ness of unfulfilled expectations. And it is in contrast to
this all-consuming passion that he is now able to sing,
"Lord, you now dismiss your servant in peace. For my
eyes have seen your salvation." God provides him release from the fury of his intensity of purpose, which
was almost a servitude or enslavement. And he is
brought into experiencing what years later the apostle Paul describes as the "glorious freedom of the children of God" (Romans 8:21).

There is a sense that what Simeon goes on to say
in his song contradicts all he lived, hoped, and prayed
for. Looking at the Christ Child, he tells him that
God's salvation is "a light for revelation to the Gentiles and for glory to your people Israel." It is amazing that, as devoted to Jewish religious law as Simeon
apparently was, he is so open to God's salvation coming to the gentiles. Many with his background stood
against the gentiles, whom they saw not only as "pa-
gans" but also as the oppressors of the Jewish people.
The Hasidim, in their extreme nationalism, saw the
Messiah and his salvation as exclusively for the Jews.

Yet here we see Simeon remarkably open to salvation
for all people. Obviously, he has been given a new
and fuller perspective on God's divine intent.

This experience of seeing the Christ Child pressed
home the point to Simeon that God would not send
him away with an unfulfilled hope. He knew in a new
and deeper way that God cares for us, and that God
is good to his word. God has been faithful to the
promise he made to Simeon. And not only to Simeon:
God has been faithful to each individual in this world,
gentile and Jew alike. The experience of seeing the
Christ Child indelibly impressed on Simeon's heart
that God's most basic characteristic, unlike the sea
that doesn't seem to care if we sink or float, is that he
wishes everyone well and is at work toward that end.
Simeon sings of the grace of God as demonstrated by
his "giving-ness"; God's desire is to give to all abun-
dantly. When Simeon tried to take it all into his own
hands, it limited his view and experience of God's
goodness.

The spirit in which Simeon sings demonstrates for
us that this new revelation of God's character brought
him tremendous security, an inner calm. He also experienced a cessation of the intensity and enslavement
of living in the future, and a freedom from the deter-
minedness that had accompanied him all his life. Realizing that God is taking care of the divine purposes,
and that those purposes are entirely good and are for
all people, brought to Simeon a relaxed disposition —

a sense of liberation. He was shown that, at its heart, life is not about doing the right thing or fulfilling religious laws, but instead about being God's cherished creation.

Simeon was released to a new kind of life: a life of peace in his deepest part. This is why he can sing, "For my eyes have seen *your salvation.*" Throughout his gospel, Luke closely connects the concept of peace with salvation, which in Luke's understanding infers the richness of the Hebrew word *shalom,* meaning the "positive blessing of God in all its many aspects." This is, of course, what the passing of the peace is all about during the service of Holy Communion. As we say to someone, "God's peace be with you," we are asking God's blessing on others in the fullest measure. In essence, Simeon is saying, "I am released because I have seen God's peace and salvation, the many aspects of the positive blessing of God." Perhaps for the first time in his life he could understand the value, depth, and joy of the present moment, what the author Spencer Johnson in his children's classic by the same title refers to as "the precious present." This is the "now" of which Simeon sings.

Simeon's experience echoes what another once-driven, restless man named Augustine experienced about four hundred years later. A North African Berber, who lived in what is now the Arab country of Algeria, Augustine wrote in his autobiographical *Confessions,* "Thou hast touched me and I have been

translated into thy peace." Simeon, with a new perspective on and revelation of God, was likewise
touched and departed in God's peace, released to a
new kind of life.

The Paradox of Suffering

As Simeon's song continues, we see that what he saw,
this revelation that released him, goes even deeper.
After he blessed the child and his parents, there was
something about the mother that stopped him. Perhaps his expression changed. What he saw in Mary's
face was a long way off, but it was there so plainly he
couldn't not say it: "And a sword will pierce your own
soul too." We get the feeling that perhaps he would
have preferred to have bitten his tongue than to have
said it, but in that sacred moment he felt he had no
choice. Then he handed the baby back and departed
in a different kind of peace: a peace of depth.

This is the first reference in Luke's gospel to
Christ's suffering; it is a note of sorrow. Pointing to
the cost and pain Mary will feel because her son is
the Messiah, and what this salvation would entail,
Simeon acknowledges that life is not only sweetness
and light. The word "sword" in Simeon's statement to
Mary denotes in Greek a large sword, not the small

dagger of the time. It is a large sword that will pierce Mary's soul, one that pierces to the heart.

Simeon's release to a new kind of life of peace entailed a revelation of suffering. Once again this seems to be a contradiction to what he was living and looking for all his life, as he was waiting for the "comfort" brought by the Messiah to his people. In Rembrandt's first painting of this scene, painted in 1628 when he was only twenty-two years old, Rembrandt places the emphasis on Mary, and we can almost see the future sorrow in her face. While Simeon stares intensely into her face, Mary's hands are clasped tightly in front of her while she looks at her child, as if bracing herself for what is to come.

Life is both difficult and marvelous. Simeon, like Adam and Eve in the process of tasting the forbidden fruit, discovers that in addition to good, there is also evil. In addition to the joy of being alive, there is also the sadness and hurt of being alive. Gautama the Buddha recognized the first of the Four Noble Truths as "life is suffering." At any given moment life can be many happy things, but suffering is universal and inevitable, and to face that reality and come to terms with it is the beginning of wisdom. Simeon's song is reminding us that suffering is an undercurrent of life.

Bad times happen and good times happen; each life is a mixture of good and bad, joy and suffering. For whatever reason, sorrow, hurt, and suffering seem to go with the territory of being human. We

carry them about with us the way a turtle carries its
shell. Suffering is one of the homes we live in. It
seems that much of life is the process of discovering
pain, and then of trying to come to terms with it, attempting to figure out how to deal with it in order to
survive. One writer describes suffering as the "tears
of things."

In Simeon's story we are also told that there was
an elderly woman named Anna at the temple. She
was one who had known deep sorrow, widowed after
only seven years of marriage, and remaining single
for the rest of her life, now being eighty-four years
old. Even Jesus himself, as the Scriptures say, was
"acquainted with grief." Certainly he was dealt plenty
of it during his thirty-some years on this planet.

Simeon seems to be musing about a fresh perspective on the *paradox of suffering.* In his statement to
Mary, he is saying that the greatest circumstance of
suffering in this world will bring about the greatest
miracle of peace that has ever taken place. And this
miracle of peace continues to occur in our lives and in
lives all over the world. Suffering takes us from experiencing the depths, to living *in* the depths, to living
out of the depths. And while one cannot survive in the
depths for too long, it is there that somehow the
pearls are found.

When the worst finally happens, or almost happens, the paradox is that a kind of peace follows.
After passing beyond grief, beyond terror, moving all

but beyond hope, it is there in that wilderness that for the first time in our lives we catch sight of something of what it must be like to know God most fully, when there is nothing else left. It may be only a glimpse, but it is like stumbling on fresh water in the desert. It is loving God and seeing God because there is almost nothing else to love or see.

I am reminded of one of the most refreshing of experiences, in the Great Sand Sea, near the oasis of Siwa in the Western Desert of Egypt. On one unbearably hot afternoon, with nothing but rolling hills of fine white sand in view for miles and miles from our four-wheel drive vehicle, we came across a large, freshwater spring. It was impossible to resist the urge to jump into the cool, crystal-clear water literally in the middle of nowhere. As the only body of water around, this pond was irresistibly inviting, and served to invigorate as nothing else could in the blistering desert.

Some of the most tragic stories in the Middle East today are told by those who have lost everything because of the war in Iraq. I recall meeting with an Iraqi Christian whose family had lived for centuries in Baghdad, members of the historic Chaldean Catholic Church. He and his family had to escape from the intense religious persecution resulting from the war, so they left their beautiful home and all their family and friends and went first to Jordan and then to Egypt. He shared with me a moment of insight when, having literally lost all, he picked up a little chipped glass bead that he saw in the street. Holding it, he declared that his suffering had shown him the "pearl in the depths," referring to his personal experience of the faithfulness of God.

In Cairo we have thousands of Sudanese refugees who have fled the intense civil war in their country taking place over the last two decades between the predominately Arab north and the African south. These refugees have gone through tremendous suffering on every side. Most of them have lost members of their immediate family through horrific circumstances. Yet when I talk with them, the predominant impression with which I am always left is their deep and contagious joy in the midst of their hardship. One Sudanese bishop wears a cross made from the scrap metal of a downed MIG jet that bombed their villages. The cross has been shaped into four small MIG jets colliding into one another to form a cross. When asked why he wears that cross, his response is, "Because it is a reminder for us that it has been at the greatest point of devastation in our lives that we have experienced God's salvation most clearly."

Perhaps that is why the Russian novelist Leo Tolstoy once said, "It is by those who have suffered that the world has been advanced." Certainly it was Tolstoy's own state of suffering that led him to become a follower of Christ. Simeon, in his few heart-wrenching words to Mary, is also saying that the truest and

most lasting peace can be found in and through the
greatest suffering. Perhaps this is what the apostle
Paul meant when he wrote to a small group in
Philippi that God's peace "passes all understanding."
Simeon sings of this special refinement of sorrow: a
sorrow that leads to the deepest and most beautiful
calm. We are enabled to ride through the storms of
life because we know that the paradox of suffering
betokens a reality beyond the storm more precious
than we can imagine.

Perhaps another poem of William Blake, *Auguries
of Innocence*, may help us to understand this paradox of
suffering.

> Man was made for joy and woe,
> And when this we rightly know,
> Thro' the world we safely go.

Simeon understands that this Christ Child did not
exist to spare us the indignities of a wounded creation. Through him we have life in the midst of life's
wounds, and can live fully and hopefully, not in some
fantastic never-never land not yet arrived, but in the
ambiguous reality here and now. Which is why
Blake's thoughtful poem continues:

> Joy and woe are woven fine,
> A clothing for the soul divine.
> Under every grief and pine
> Runs a joy with silken twine.

Blake was very aware that good and evil, joy and suffering are the two poles between which the current of life passes, and that paradoxically they are able to generate a divine spark within us.

Kahlil Gibran, the early twentieth-century Arab mystic whose background was in the historic Maronite Catholic Church of Lebanon, is frequently referred to as the "William Blake of the twentieth century." While he is best known in the West for his book *The Prophet*, Gibran also wrote an inspirational short story titled *The Tempest*. The story is about a young man who visits a monk in a cave up in the Lebanese mountains who has supposedly "escaped the world," in order to learn the monk's secrets. However, when a massive thunderstorm begins, the monk walks out into the middle of it to spend the night, rather than taking refuge in the cave as the man expected he would. As the monk heads into the storm, his parting words to the visitor, who chooses to stay in the cave, are, "I hope you teach yourself to love the tempest."[12]

So every year, as the Advent season draws to a close and we prepare to celebrate Christmas, we are presented with both a *challenge* and an *invitation*. This child, born into our world, made possible for Simeon not just a new way of understanding life but a new way of living. Seeing the Christ Child gave Simeon a fresh revelation of God and the way God uses suffering. This revelation is one that each of us can experience this Advent. The child in Simeon's arms gives us a new ability to live a new kind of life, where both living in the present and living with suffering are immeasurably deepened. It is a life lived in peace in the innermost part of our being. The two names given by Isaiah for this Messiah child say it all: the Prince of Peace, the Wonderful Counselor. Because he is our Wonderful Counselor, he can also be our Prince of Peace.

Once again, this truth is poignantly reflected in Rembrandt's life. Following his death, there was found in his studio an unfinished painting of Simeon in the temple, a work that exudes a mystical sense of hope. As we have noted, this scene had preoccupied Rembrandt since his earliest days; he had previously painted it three times in an attempt to capture the emotional power of this story of an elderly man holding the Christ Child after years of longing and waiting. By the end of his own life, Rembrandt had personally gone through significant suffering: the deaths of three of his children, his mother, and then his wife, Saskia; personal bankruptcy; and an increasing lack of public appreciation for his style of painting. The last few years of his life were especially difficult. The difference in this fourth and unfinished painting is that for Simeon's face, Rembrandt now painted his own. Perhaps he too saw what Simeon saw and finally understood what it meant to be released to live and enjoy God's peace, even in the midst of suffering.

Endnotes

1. Jan L. Richardson, *Night Visions: Searching the Shadows of Advent and Christmas* (Cleveland: United Church Press, 1998).

2. Dag Hammarskjöld, *Markings* (New York: Alfred A. Knopf, 1964), 46.

3. G. K. Chesterton, *Autobiography* (London: Burns Oates, 1937), 94–95.

4. Flannery O'Connor, *Mystery and Manners* (New York: Farrar, Straus and Giroux, 1969), 118.

5. C. S. Lewis, *Letters to Malcolm: Chiefly on Prayer* (New York: Harcourt, Inc., 1964), 89–90.

6. Quoted in Roland H. Bainton, *Here I Stand: A Life of Martin Luther* (Signet, 1955), 288.

7. C. S. Lewis, *The Weight of Glory and Other Addresses* (San Francisco: HarperSanFrancisco, 1976), 26, 38–39.

8. A. J. Appasamy, *Sundar Singh* (Cambridge: James Clark & Co., 2002), 134.

9. C. S. Lewis, *The Last Battle* (New York: Macmillan Publishing Co., 1970), 140.

10. C. S. Lewis, *Perelandra* (New York: Macmillan Publishing Co., 1965), 144.

11. Dietrich Bonhoeffer, *Letters From Prison* (Beaverton, Oregon: Touchstone Press, 1997).

12. Kahlil Gibran, *A Treasury of Wisdom: A Collection of the Works of Kahlil Gibran* (Kent, UK: Grange Book/Axiom Publishing, 2001), 127.

About the Author

PAUL-GORDON CHANDLER is an American Episcopal priest and interfaith advocate. He grew up in West Africa (Senegal), and has lived and worked extensively throughout the Islamic world with churches, faith-based publishing groups, and relief and development agencies.

He is the author of *Pilgrims of Christ on the Muslim Road: Exploring a New Path Between Two Faiths* and *God's Global Mosaic.*

Paul-Gordon Chandler is married with two children.

The author may be contacted through his website:
www.paulgordonchandler.com.

About the Artist

DANIEL BONNELL graduated from the Atlanta
College of Art, where he studied painting under the
renowned New York abstract expressionist painter
Ed Ross. His postgraduate studies were under the
tutelage of the legendary photographer Ansel Adams
and the renowned designer Milton Glaser. His greatest teaching came from a French Dominican monk,
Père Couturier, who ushered such great painters as
Henri Matisse and Fernand Léger into creating sacred art.

Bonnell's work is found in private collections,
churches, and cathedrals around the world; his well-
known *Images on Christ* series had its inaugural exhi-
bition at St. Paul's Cathedral in London. A collection
of his paintings has been published in *The Road Home:
A Journey in Art and Music* by Garth Hewitt and he is
a featured artist in Alister McGrath's book *The Chris-*

tian Vision of God. The White Stone Gallery in Philadelphia and The Hayden-Hays Gallery at the Broadmoor in Colorado Springs represent his gallery work.

Daniel Bonnell's work may be viewed and he may be contacted at these websites:
www.BonnellArt.com and www.iocproject.com

Printed in the USA
CPSIA information can be obtained
at www.ICGtesting.com
JSHW012002151123
52157JS00014B/692

9 780898 690699